Robbert Hartog

A LIFETIME OF CHANGING LIVES

SHANNON TEAHEN

Robbert Hartog

A LIFETIME OF CHANGING LIVES

SHANNON TEAHEN

A publication of the University of Waterloo, 2009

Library and Archives Canada Cataloguing in Publication

Teahen, Shannon
Robbert Hartog : a lifetime of changing lives / Shannon Teahen.

Includes bibliographical references and index.
ISBN 978-0-9682827-4-8

1. Hartog, Robbert, 1919-2008. 2. Businessmen--Canada--Biography.
3. Philanthropists--Ontario--Midland--Biography. 4. Civic leaders-- Ontario--
Midland--Biography. 5. Directors of corporations--Canada--Biography.
6. Wye Marsh Wildlife Centre--Biography. 7. Midland (Ont.)--Biography.
I. Title.

HV28.H37T43 2009   338.092   C2009-906203-8

The inclusion of so many personal and family photographs has enhanced the look and feel of this book. We are especially grateful to so many who shared their personal photographs and who gave us permission to use them in this book. The majority of the photographs are from private collections or from Robbert's personal files. Robbert's sister, Rose-Marjan Hartog graciously permitted us to reprint rare family photographs in her possession. John Bell, Gary Gray, Bob Hutt, Hudson Leavens, Kyle Nash, Rittichai Jantayavichit, and Ken Woods sent along interesting images pertaining to various aspects of Robbert's life. We are also grateful to several institutions for permission to use their photos, including the University of Waterloo, Shore Tilbe Irwin and Partners, and the YMCA of Simcoe/ Muskoka. Other photos are from the author's private collection.

First Published in 2009 by
University of Waterloo
200 University Avenue West
Waterloo, Ontario, Canada N2L 3G1

Design and Production by Sue Breen and Chris McCorkindale,
McCorkindale Advertising & Design

Historical Consultant: Kenneth McLaughlin, *Distinguished Professor Emeritus, University of Waterloo*

Copy Editors Kenneth McLaughlin and Ruth Taylor

Printed in Canada by Friesens Corporation, Altona, Manitoba, Canada

Contents

Foreword

In life, you are fortunate, blessed really, if you run into a person like Robbert Hartog. Other than my family, Robbert has had the most influence on my life.

When I first met him in 1984, Robbert had recently sold his business and I had just begun an investment counselling company. We had some difficulty finding a time to meet and his favourite story was that I kept changing appointments on him because I was trying to land a bigger fish! When we finally met, Robbert became a client of ours by sending a cheque for $1 million — in the mail! My secretary, Mary Pritchard, almost fainted when she opened the envelope. That began a relationship that spanned almost a quarter of a century — till the day he passed away in 2008.

Less than a year after Robbert became my client, an opportunity to acquire control of Fairfax arose. Without hesitation, Robbert backed me when we refinanced the company and he became a board member and chairman of the Audit Committee, positions he retained till he retired in 2007. Other than for donations, he never sold any of his Fairfax shares.

When we acquired control of Fairfax, I was 35 years old, had never been on a board, and was pretty naïve about business. Robbert, a bachelor, devoted extraordinary amounts of time to me and to Fairfax, both at the outset and continuously over the next 25 years. He was reachable at any time, seven days a week — and at Fairfax we never made any important decisions without his blessing.

Robbert had created a wonderful company called Waltec which for a nearly 40-year span became the largest plumbing supplies company in Canada — before he sold it to Masco (Emco, in Canada). He loved to share the benefits of his experience in building a successful business with people like me, and also with charitable organizations — particularly the YMCA and the Boy Scouts of Canada. He was a keen volunteer in CESO (Canadian Executive Service Organization) and travelled far and wide to help businesses in less developed countries. When we asked him why he did this, he said simply that he was blessed and this was his small way of giving back to others what he had received. As you will read in a detailed excerpt in the book, as one outstanding example of this, the Thai family and Jaguar Industries are ever grateful for Robbert's commitment and friendship.

Robbert loved Canada and he felt that in Canada we had the best of both worlds — a free enterprise society together with compassion for the less fortunate. Anything was possible in Canada — as he demonstrated in his life. He was an entrepreneur who worked hard in all that he did. He encouraged me and others to dream big and was always optimistic about the future — but brutally honest in facing reality. He once told me that his grandfather had said to him that truth is always absolute — if you begin to shade it, you are sliding down a very slippery slope. Robbert did not shade the truth and he always focused on doing the right thing.

While Robbert spent enormous time supporting community organizations and was extremely generous to them, he abhorred any recognition. When we celebrated his birthdays over the years at Fairfax, he allowed us not more than two minutes to praise him! In fact, I did not know till recently that he had won the highest awards granted by both Scouting and the YMCA — the only person in Canada or the United States who had ever done so!

Robbert was a self-made man who achieved great success while always acting with the highest integrity. He was a wonderful mentor to me (and to countless others) and I used to call him my godfather. Robbert made a lasting impact on many organizations, but, I believe, on none as significantly as he did on Fairfax. I am delighted that Shannon Teahen has written this book on Robbert's life. I know it will inspire many people to dream big and to achieve their dreams while scrupulously guarding their integrity.

Prem Watsa
Chairman, Fairfax Financial Holdings
Chancellor, The University of Waterloo

Preface

A smile of pride graced Robbert Hartog's face as he made his way to the front of the large hall, reflecting on his lifetime of experiences. Robbert stood poised in a black tuxedo, his short, robust figure facing the front of the room. His name was read out and he stepped towards Canadian Governor General Jeanne Sauvé, who was regal in her deep purple dress. She pinned the Order of Canada to his lapel as she lauded his achievements. When he stepped back from the Governor General, Robbert's smile remained.

On October 30, 1985, Robbert Hartog was one of 48 Canadians awarded the Royal Order of Canada at an investiture ceremony at Rideau Hall in Ottawa. This was his country's highest tribute for his distinguished service to Canada, to his fellow citizens and to humanity at large. Robbert attended the ceremony with his friend Guusje Parks, who said the evening was "a wonderful experience." Robbert was extremely honoured by Canada's recognition of his services and he proudly wore on his lapel a miniature replica of the medal given to members of the Order. Robbert later remarked, "I do not like honours and awards, but I also happen to be a fierce Canadian nationalist, and therefore, I was really pleased to receive the Order of Canada."

Robbert receiving his Order of Canada medal from Canadian Governor General Jeanne Sauvé.

Photo © Estate of John Evans Photography, Ottawa

Robbert's nomination for the award was spearheaded by a group of his former Sea Scouts, and supported by a broad cross-section of Canadians, as described by the Honourable Donald S. Macdonald, a former president of the Privy Council and Minister of Finance, who was also involved in the Boy Scout movement. One of Robbert's Scouts, Larry Halliday, began the campaign by collecting letters supporting him from friends, as well as from community members in his small town of Midland, Ontario. The words of appreciation for Robbert's dedicated service, from a long list of Canadians from different walks of life, speak volumes about a man who gave so much of himself while demanding little or no credit for his actions.

> Mr. Hartog is one of those remarkable individuals with super-abundant energy and a quite remarkable ability to achieve a variety of things in a limited amount of time. He has been a thoroughly good citizen, and I think his recognition by way of the Order of Canada for these services to Canadian youth is one that would be welcomed by a broad spectrum of the Canadian community.
>
> — *The Honourable Donald S. Macdonald*

> His contribution over many years at the local, national and worldwide levels is documented and can be measured. But what is difficult to document, because he is a very private person in this regard, is his impact on a succession of generations of young Canadians on a one-to-one basis. If the rippling effect were to be put in place, there would be a veritable tidal wave on its way. Indeed, over the years, working with various volunteer organizations, there is no one we have ever been exposed to who has dedicated so much of himself and his resources to the young men and women who were fortunate enough to cross his path. He gave them his trust and made them aware of his faith in their potential as productive members of society.
>
> — *Thomas H. Gibson, Betty A. Gibson, and*
> *Thomas S. Gibson, Friends of Robbert Hartog*

My first acquaintance with Mr. Hartog was in 1952, when as a 12-year-old, I became a member of a Scout troop organized and headed by Mr. Hartog. Through the next formative five years, under his steward-ship, we matured and can trace many of our positive and community-oriented attitudes to his influence. His effect on the group of boys who started in that original troop has been so profound that we still get together annually with him, and many of us have served in Scouting as leaders over the years. Again having been out of Scouting for a number of years, I personally have become involved again and constantly think to myself, What would Robbert have done in this particular situation? My memories as a boy are so happy and vivid that I strive to create the same atmosphere that he created so many years ago.

— *Steve Glogowski, Former Scout*

Robbert Hartog has had a fine and lasting influence on the quality of life of the youth of this area. Robbert moved to Midland in 1962 and, through his work with older Scouts, soon understood their needs and frustrations. At this time he was also a director of our YMCA. Robbert recognized the inadequacy of our lovely old downtown Y facility. In a small community, there is an even greater need for an excellent centre to serve young people. Robbert Hartog understood this and inspired the Y board and the community to undertake what we feared was an impossible dream. From the steering committee stage through to the completion of the building, Robbert was a quiet tower of strength both with his business and organizational ability and with his considerable financial support.

— *Jean Hartman, Past President of Midland YMCA*

His marvellous, quick understanding of everything and everyone, his ability to quickly grasp implications, his perspicacity, are gifts that have altruistically touched thousands — especially in their youth — and their young. Not only has he benefited organizations such as Scouting, the YMCA, the Red Cross, Georgian College, the YPO, CIPH, the Canadian Plumbing Industry and many others of which I am characteristically unaware, but countless individuals as well. I always receive a comment, a note or a phone call of understanding, whether a disappointment be large or small, sometimes so small that I am warmed that it was detected, let alone acknowledged.

— *Hudson Leavens, Former Scout and Employee*

Robbert is still a staunch ally of the Friends of Wye Marsh and continues to serve on the board of directors. A few years ago, upon returning from a trip to the Amazon River and its famous wetlands, he mentioned that he had gained a global perspective for the local importance of wetland communities like the Wye Marsh. This extensive background in world travel, combined with his vision for business, conservation, fundraising, and community events, was a perfect combination for the growth of the Wye Marsh Wildlife Centre to its present position as a natural history centre of national prominence.

— *Bob Whittam, Executive Director of the Board of the Wye Marsh*

Robbert is also a keen, astute and successful business man. When I started my own business he was always very liberal with advice, suggestions, etc., — whether or not they were sought! His present standing in the business community of Canada and many other places in the world is a tribute to his abilities. Although born in Holland, Robbert has become a true Canadian in every sense of the word. Very few native Canadians have contributed as much to our country as has Robbert — businesswise, politically or helping our fellow Canadians. His sphere of influence has been felt in many different areas — and I believe the country has been the better for his being here.

— *Garfield Lorriman, Friend of Robbert Hartog*

I am one of the many who have benefited from being introduced to the challenges and pleasures of life in the Canadian wilderness through many canoe trips, boating trips and other outdoor expeditions led by Robbert Hartog. On these outdoor adventures, he has taught young Canadians from various communities such skills as wilderness survival, cooking, fitness and effective teamwork. His example inspired respect and appreciation for the beauty and pleasure of Canada's outdoors.

— *Evan Monkman, Former Scout*

Many other people whose lives were touched by Robbert echoed these words of appreciation; the outpouring of support overwhelmed him. In January 1985 Robbert wrote, "When I heard last November what 'was going to happen' and how so many people had been involved, I was not only most pleasantly surprised, but also felt that my old 'intelligence sense' had obviously faded! While I am absolutely convinced that many other people deserve an award much more than I, I must admit that it is an honour and, with the many expressions of good friends, a real privilege." Robbert's service had already exceeded what most citizens could achieve in a lifetime. Over the next two decades, Robbert only increased his service to his local and global community.

Acknowledgments

I am very fortunate to have been brought into Robbert Hartog's life, and although I never had the pleasure of meeting Robbert, through the stories of his family, friends, and business associates, I quickly became acquainted with his generous spirit and numerous accomplishments. Access to many of his personal files and photographs provided me with the opportunity to review Robbert's letters and his correspondence and thereby to incorporate his voice in the book. The legacy that he left with those whom he knew made it easy for me to conduct almost one hundred oral interviews with willing participants from all areas of Robbert's life. Space does not allow me to thank each one here, but a list of names of those whom I interviewed is appended to this book.

I would particularly like to thank Reinhart Weber for his support of this project from its inception. His guidance throughout the process and his personal knowledge of and friendship with Robbert over so many years was extremely valuable and greatly appreciated. Robbert's family: Rose-Marjan Hartog, Ronald Schokking, J.J. Schokking, and many of his nieces and nephews with whom I had the pleasure of corresponding, added insight into Robbert's personality and his role within the family. I am honoured to have Prem Watsa introduce the book with his Foreword. Hudson Leavens aided me in various aspects of the book, especially the business timeline and photographs. Fred Hacker provided an eloquent testimonial in the Postscript of the book. Researching Robbert's life provided me with the wonderful opportunity to travel to meet his family and friends abroad. It was a pleasure to know his childhood friend Thys Rissedela and Robbert's cousin Huug van Dantzig and his wife Marianne in Holland. Their kindness and contributions to the book are especially appreciated. Thank you also to Akachai Jantayavichit, Suchitra Niramyakul, Rittichai Jantayavichit, Rasamee Jantayavichit, and the staff of Jaguar Industries in Thailand. No wonder Robbert returned to Bangkok so often to visit. Your hospitality and enthusiasm for this book made my trip there invaluable.

At the University of Waterloo, President David Johnston, Vice President, External Relations, Meg Beckel, and Jeannie Watt assisted me throughout the process. Sue Breen and Chris McCorkindale at McCorkindale Advertising and Design in Waterloo created a stunning layout for the book. I had much help during my research for the book, translating documents, transcribing interviews, conducting background research, and forming a layout of the pictures. Anna Kleinschmidt, William Pensaert, Donna Lang, Dave Kielstra, Sarah Morse and Becky McDowell were there for me. The Historical Advisory Committee members: Dr. Kenneth McLaughlin, Dr. Whitney Lackenbauer, and Dr. Ryan Touhey provided a critical review of the manuscript. The chair of the committee and my supervisor from the beginning to the end of this project, Dr. Kenneth McLaughlin, recently named as a *Distinguished Professor Emeritus* of history at the University of Waterloo, brought insight, patience and encouragement. From the beginning, his belief in my ability to see this project through was a true motivation.

I am indebted to my family and friends for their enduring support. You have contributed to my enthusiasm for the project and I am thrilled to share Robbert's story with you. I would like to thank my brother Jonathan Teahen for his positive words when I needed them the most. Thank you Holly Teahen, my mother, for your compassion and encouragement that drove me forward. To my father, David Teahen, I am grateful for your patience and endurance throughout this process. I would especially like to thank my fiancé, Kyle Nash, who supported me throughout all aspects of this project. Thank you for being my travel partner, my sounding board, and my constant source of faith. My appreciation for you is unending. Finally I would like to thank Robbert Hartog. His inspirational life made this book possible. Thank you for influencing generations through your determination, good works, and kind spirit. I have learned a great deal from you that I will always hold dear. Any errors in the book are mine alone.

A Family Photo Album of Robbert's Childhood

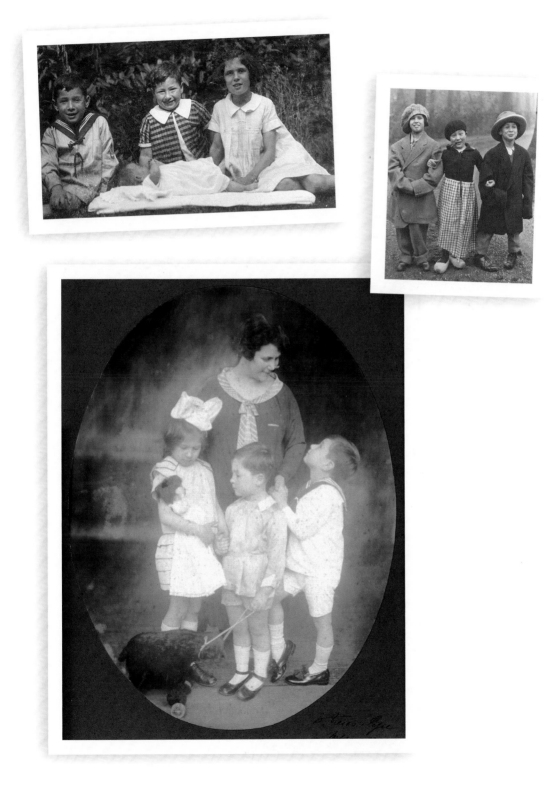

CHAPTER ONE

The Formative Years

Robbert Hartog's life of service and success is born of a rich history. Although it was his fellow Canadians who championed him for his achievements, Robbert came from Dutch ancestry. He was born on January 28, 1919, in Nijmegen, The Netherlands, to Arthur and Jeanette (formerly Catz) Hartog. His older sister, Ellen, was born on January 1, 1917. His younger brother, Dolf, was born November 4, 1920, and his younger sister, Rose-Marjan, was born March 29, 1926. His father, Arthur, was the tenth child born, of eleven, to Hartog Hartog and Marianne Van den Bergh.

Robbert's grandfather, Hartog Hartog, began his career as a butcher. In 1872 he moved from the small village of Heesch to Oss, where he started a slaughterhouse. During the first few years, he moved his firm several times and later was able to extend his business to related activities such as fat-rendering and the production of soap from animal fats. Over the years, he worked with the help of his family relatives, the Van Zwanenbergs (also butchers) and the Van den Berghs (who made butter). His firm moved once more, this time closer to the Oss railway, and was

Left to right: Dolf, Ellen, Rose-Marjan, and Robbert Hartog.

The Hartog family enjoying a ski vacation. Robbert is pictured third from the right.

situated next to the Van Zwanenberg operation. The owners of the two firms were related, but they were also in competition. In 1893 Hartog began to capitalize on the expansive British meat market by exporting to Great Britain, where he had secured an entrance when his son Simon went to London and worked for a former agent of Hartog's. The sideline of manufacturing animal fats brought the Hartog business into the profitable development of a new product, margarine, which came to play an important role in the food industry. In 1929 the Margarine Union took over the entire Hartog family firm. The second generation, the five sons of Hartog, negotiated a good price for the company and it was sold to what would later become Unilever. Two brothers, Jacob and Robbert's father, Arthur, gained high positions in Unilever (which was founded shortly after the sale and would later be known as Lever Brothers).

A primary school photo of Robbert (second row, far left) and his classmates.

Robbert's grandfather's and his father's success in business gave him a childhood filled with luxuries that were uncommon in interwar Europe. Robbert's sister, Rose-Marjan, recalls that they lived comfortably, and acknowledged that they were privileged, and she said this came with a responsibility, such as giving back — something that always interested Robbert and that shaped his life. The family moved frequently to beautiful large homes. According to Rose-Marjan, the family moved in 1924/5 to Ubbergen, The Netherlands, where they lived from

1925 to 1929. There, Robbert attended a private primary school called Nuts. His classmate and childhood friend, Thys Risselada, remembers Robbert as a very keen student, very clear in his statements, but who did not need to be first in the group. Because of his knowledge, however, he often came at the top of his class. In those early days, Thys recalled, Robbert was never late; in fact, he was always early and proud of his punctuality, another trait that he would carry throughout his life. The family moved to Versailles, France, when Arthur was transferred there in 1929. They lived at 9 Boulevard de la Reine — a beautiful home just outside the gates of the Palace of Versailles. During his time in France, Robbert first came into contact with the Scouting movement.

In 1934, in the midst of the Great Depression, the Hartogs moved back to The Netherlands to an affluent suburb of Den Haag called Wassenaar. They lived in a tall white house surrounded by lush trees and a sprawling lawn. The house had large windows and several patios. According to Thys, Arthur had renovations done to the house and also added a tennis court and a stable. Robbert and his brother Dolf attended high school at Nederlands Lyceum in Wassenaar, where Robbert was introduced to the classic languages of Latin and Greek. Rose-Marjan explained that students learn French in grade 3 or 4 of primary school. In high school, students learn German in grade 9. They also study English in school. Robbert had a strong Dutch accent throughout his life, but his command of multiple languages can be attributed to this educational background.

Robbert left The Netherlands to study economics at the École Libre des Sciences Politiques in Paris, one of a handful of elite educational institutions in France whose graduates went on to form France's ruling class

The Hartogs resided in this house in Wassenaar in the late 1930s. The home was damaged by a fire in the 1960s and was remodeled into apartments that resemble its original construction.

in business and government. At the École Libre des Sciences Politiques each country had its own house for residents, so Robbert stayed in the Dutch house. In his records, Robbert kept his class notes. He had Law exam notes titled Written Practice/Repetition of Political Economy, as well as study notes in English and French on various political and economic subjects, including the electrical industry, the textile industry, the agricultural industry, and price cost. In Written Practice/Repetition of Financial Management, Robbert's notes cover personal and transferable fortune, fixed revenue values, state value or private, large business, collective working-class action, and contemporary finance. From 1939 to 1940 Robbert worked at Lever Brothers (formerly Unilever) as the assistant to the director in the Treasury Department.

Robbert completed his thesis titled "The Usefulness of Exchange Control in Wartime" in June 1940 at the École Libre des Sciences Politiques, but its publication was delayed because of wartime emergencies. In the preface, Robbert thanked his professors de Peyster, de Blank, and Angeloglou for their time and counsel. He explained in his thesis that exchange controls are types of controls imposed by a government to restrict

Robbert (third row, far left) in his later schooling years.

the amount of foreign or local currency that can be purchased or sold. "It is evident," he wrote, "that the term control implies interference in relation to others. As regards to the Exchange Control, we must expect attacks on liberty. However, these must be considered as being the inevitable corollary of the system." It was no little irony that during the late 1930s, exchange control had gained particular celebrity and Robbert sought to understand the sudden interest in it. He intended to distinguish between the motives that drove the Exchange Control in war or peace, and to outline the experiences in France and England, concluding that the very fact of resorting to Exchange Control indicates a rupture of balance. He believed that it should always be possible to resolve an economic crisis without interventionism. Exchange Control should only be accepted as a temporary and exceptional measure. On the other hand, he argued the need for Exchange Control is born from a period of war, an extra-economic period, and thus, such controls must disappear with the end of the hostilities. Ultimately, the important thing is to return to a regime of freedom.

The publication of Robbert's thesis was delayed until 1941 due to political events in Europe.

Robbert believed in the market forces, not the heavy hand of government intervention in economic affairs. He said, "Exchange Control is definitely harmful; it can be thought of as an awkward, but useful remedy. Its institution is, however, an economic arm in times of war and struggle for the Defence of the Nation." The ideas in Robbert's thesis forecast his own philosophy of business.

In 1941 he sent his thesis to various banks for review. H. Groeneveld, head of a department in the Ministry of Finance in London, agreed with many of his points and told him, "You were lucky to be able to complete your project in Paris because the atmosphere isn't so calm there since June of last year [1940]." Groenveld added, "The English-French monetary co-operation has changed to French-German co-operation. The trade regulations shall become one-sided in favour of the Germans."

With the outbreak of the Second World War in 1939, as a Jewish family, the Hartogs were in danger if they stayed in Europe. As the Nazis advanced on France and The Netherlands (which was a neutral country) the Hartogs were forced to flee from their home. During the war, three-quarters of the Jews in Holland were deported to extermination camps and killed by the Nazis. Rose-Marjan recalled that half of her mother's side of the family perished in the Holocaust. Many on her father's side died

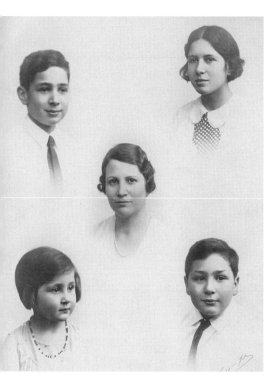

A family portrait of (top left to right) Robbert, Ellen, Jeanette, Rose-Marjan, and Dolf.

as well. She explained that there is an existential difference between Canadian and European perceptions of the war: people outside of Europe did not experience the conflict personally — to them it was abstract, but not to the Hartogs.

Unfortunately, the neutral Dutch had no concerted plans for the defence of their nation, except to blow up bridges and dyke systems should the Germans invade. The army was poorly armed and trained, although it comprised 400,000 men. Such were the Dutch defenders that met invading German forces on May 10, 1940. Germany's fuehrer, Adolf Hitler, immediately sought to integrate The Netherlands into the German political and economic nation. Hundreds of thousands of Dutch citizens were deported to Germany for employment as slave labour. On May 14, 1940, Germany bombed Rotterdam and destroyed most of the city's port and ship docks. Over 40 per cent of the city was shattered. This onslaught forced the Dutch to surrender.

Robbert's mother and his two sisters fled Holland in June 1940. They were able to escape because of Robbert's father's prominent role in Unilever. According to Robbert's cousin, Huug van Dantzig, Jeanette, whom he described as a "strong" mother, wanted to go by boat to England, but she had a premonition that something was not right with the departing boat. Instead, they travelled by train to southern France. She was extremely fortunate, as German forces torpedoed the boat on which they were to have travelled. Next, they took a small boat to Canada and settled in Toronto. In the meantime, Unilever sent Arthur to South Africa, and later to Shanghai and Hong Kong. The Japanese entered the war and occupied Hong Kong on December 25, 1941. Arthur Hartog was taken prisoner and released after two years in captivity. He was eventually sent to Toronto to establish a Unilever office in exile, should London fall to the Nazis. Robbert's brother Dolf was a resistance fighter trapped in Nazi-occupied Holland. He was captured and spent 4 years (April 1941-April 1945) in a German concentration camp. He was liberated at Mauthausen-Ebensee, where he was imprisoned after the "death-march" from Auschwitz. He then acted as an English translator for the troops. The war also took its toll on the relationship between Robbert's parents, who were later divorced.

Robbert had been in Paris when the war broke out, completing his final exam the day before the Germans entered Paris in the spring of 1940. That June, France was divided into occupied territory and unoccupied territory (known as Vichy). French citizens needed passes to move from one region to the other. In 1940 Robbert was issued a temporary card of passage by the French Republic and was permitted to circulate in all the interior zone departments for commercial business and to use all forms of locomotion. After the war, Robbert did not talk a lot about his experiences, but many close to him speculated that he was part of the underground during his time in Paris. As the war raged on, he fled southward out of Paris and spent the remainder of 1940 going between the south of France and the somewhat flexible border between German-occupied France and Vichy France, helping people cross the lines. He worked with the Scouts to resettle people from the north of France (internal refugees). Rose-Marjan said that Robbert did not leave until that was finished, and according to Robbert's understated account, "The borders were flexible, attitudes were flexible, the underground was not that well organized." Thys said that, on one occasion, German forces caught Robbert when he was trying to cross into Vichy France. The mayor of the village saw what happened and knew Robbert through Scouting and helped set him free. When asked in an interview later in life if what he did at that time was dangerous, Robbert replied, "When you're 21 you don't look at danger."

In a notepad, Robbert recorded his observations on wartime France. He left himself reminders or tasks to accomplish, such as "take another look at the maps of the occupied zone in France." Near the end of the notebook are several addresses of people all over France. Underneath the names he wrote, "leads for VICHY." He also mentioned visas needed to leave the country and he listed the United States, the Netherlands, Portugal, and Spain. Among Robbert's records he had a copy of *Free France*, a daily publication that aimed for a peaceful relationship between the French and the English. Among his notes Robbert also kept several aged handwritten poems in Dutch. One reads: *If Rob were once to marry / and searched among all those women / someone who wants him / someone who can really help him / always be on time / and early to breakfast / … Ask all your friends for such a woman / but so many girls are excluded /since the hyper-ideal /becomes abnormal.* On the side is the comment, "Is there perhaps here something for you?" He also had a number of maps in Dutch, including "Organizations Managing the Dutch Economy" and "Vital Industries."

After receiving "a few warnings," Robbert went to the south of France to begin his escape to North America. Rose-Marjan recalled that when Robbert went to Marseilles, he went to the American embassy for a visa to leave the country. They refused his entry because Robbert suffered from jaundice at the time. The clerk replied, "The yellow quota is closed," as they thought he was from Asia. Robbert's visa expired on the eighth of December, so he needed to improvise in order to stay in France. He forged the numeral one in front of the eight on his visa, making it 18 December. He then left Marseilles and travelled to Algeria, then to Morocco, then to Lisbon on the *Portuguese* S/S, and finally to New York. He arrived in Toronto on January 1, 1941. A new chapter — the life and times of Robbert Hartog was about to begin in his adopted country.

Upon his arrival, Robbert attempted to join the Canadian armed forces, but was declared unfit. "Some health reasons," he recalled. In 1941 he applied to the University of Toronto for a master's degree in political science to study economic theory, money, and corporate finance. On September 23, 1941, V.W. Bladen, from the University of Toronto Department of Political Economy, informed Robbert that the Graduate Committee of the department, had admitted him to the graduate school as an MA candidate. His registration was confirmed on November 8, 1941, for the 1941/1942 sessions. He would be required to write a short dissertation in connection with one of these courses.

During Robbert's study, the war raged on and awareness of the troubles in Europe permeated Toronto — men in uniform could be seen on campus and specialized course material was designed for military personnel. Enrolment in engineering increased, while enrolment in the arts declined, so low in 1943 that there were motions that the Arts Faculty should be

A courtyard at the rear of Hart House at the University of Toronto.

In 1942 Robbert worked at Massey-Harris, located at 915 King Street West in Toronto.

closed and that faculties unrelated to the war effort should be curtailed until peacetime. It is speculated that at some point during the war Robbert converted to the United Church of Canada.

Robbert wrote his final examinations from May 4 to 6, 1942, and was awarded his master's degree in June 1942. After graduation he worked in the head office of Massey-Harris Co. Ltd. at 915 King Street West, Toronto, as the liaison between the American company and the Canadian factories, as well as between the head office and the American factories in connection with farm machinery production and other war work.

In 1942 he frequently wrote to two of his professors — Professor Bladen and Professor Ashley. In May he wrote Ashley telling him of a throat operation he had to undergo. In the fall Robbert toyed with the idea of continuing his studies at the University of Toronto and getting a minor in mathematics.

But Robbert never returned as a student. Instead, on July 15, 1943, he enrolled in the Royal Netherlands Army. In June he had written to Major Thomas in the Personnel Selection Department in Toronto. "I have now received my draft-call from the Netherlands Army, and under these circumstances I feel that it is my duty to serve with the Netherlands Forces," he explained. "I am certain that you will understand that now that I am called up I feel that I have to give preference to the Netherlands Army." He joined the Princess Irene Brigade, which was in charge of helping rebuild the country once the war was won. Massey-Harris requested that his leave be pushed to September 1, 1943. He reported to Guelph, Ontario, to the Princess Juliana Barracks. Robbert left Canada and returned to Europe in the fall of 1943, where he was sent to London, England, and attached to the Supreme Headquarters Allied Expeditionary Force.

Robbert in his Royal Netherlands Army uniform.

Robbert was a wonderful asset to the Allied Forces with his knowledge of Dutch, French, and English, as well as his education in economics. He worked in Economic Intelligence, and due to the nature of this specialized division there are no details of his work. He was in a group of 20 who analyzed German economic data and was part of a task force designed to prepare for the invasion of Europe. Robbert said he worked "six-and-a-half days a week. I finally ended up writing the food distribution rules and price controls for Holland that would happen after liberation." In July 1944, he flew in a small plane to France while the Allied Forces were still engaged in the Normandy Campaign to reclaim territory. He moved eastward with the liberation armies, interrogating prisoners. By the winter of 1945 he was back in his hometown of Nijmegen waiting for the final Allied offensive. That winter was incredibly harsh in the Netherlands due to *Hongerwinter*, a famine caused by an embargo on food supplies that killed 18,000 people. Robbert witnessed the tragedy first-hand.

Holland was liberated on May 5, 1945. The task of rebuilding a country exhausted by war, its industry and economy in ruins, was daunting. Robbert worked for the military government. "Some Dutch university professors had been meeting all during the war and what they had in mind and the work we did paralleled," he said. "We had no problems." According to Thys, at the end of the war, Robbert also worked for the Dutch Ministry of Economic Affairs in London.

Robbert was offered the position of Assistant Deputy Minister, Reconstruction, in the postwar Dutch government. "It was a very attractive offer," he recalled. "The deputy minister was an outstanding person. But I decided I was not made for the civil service. I made up my mind to go back to Canada." He chose Canada as his home because he liked the natural environment, the space, and the people. Robbert was also offered admission to a PhD program at Harvard University. Rose-Marjan said he thought about it, but realized that he would go into an ivory tower and have no contact with the world. Robbert's intellect and analytical mind made him well suited for academia, but he decided against it.

Robbert thrived in his Rosedale neighbourhood as a Scout leader and a member of the Rosedale United Church. He lived at 31 Crescent Road and met lifelong friends during his time there. In 1949 Robbert, along with Vern Heisey, Bill Phair, Donald Deacon and Bob Telfer, initiated Mayfair in Rosedale Park, an annual fundraiser for the Rosedale/Moore Park Association. In the early years it raised funds to build a com-

Robbert and his mother, Jeanette — who is described as a strong mother with interests in music and politics.

munity centre. In 1950, Robbert was program chairman of the event. Mayfair, held the Saturday before Mother's Day in Rosedale Park, continues today and is the largest and longest running volunteer community fair in Toronto. Ruth Rowland, a friend of Robbert's from the Mayfair days, said the fair featured such events as a parade, races, and a plant booth (for young boys to buy Mother's Day presents). The main organizer carried a cane and walked around the grounds of the fair. This cane was passed along from one year to another.

Although Robbert came from privileged beginnings, the dedication he showed throughout his youth and as a young man translated to all levels of his social and business endeavours throughout his lifetime. Early on he learned the value of family, generosity, and commitment. As a young boy, Robbert worked a small job to make some money for himself and he brought the money home to Arthur. His father asked what he was going to do with the money and Robbert replied that he would save some and then buy something. "How much will you give back to others?" Arthur queried. With the help of his father, Robbert put away 20 per cent of his earnings to help others. Robbert would later say that this was an eye-opening experience for him. He could set aside a little bit and make a difference. And so he did. From that point onward, Robbert never stopped giving.

Above: The Hartog family's Rosedale home at 146 South Drive where they lived from 1940-1944.

Below: Robbert (centre) at the Mayfair with the symbolic cane carried by the main organizers.

CHAPTER TWO

The Successful Businessman

W hen Robbert Hartog returned to Canada, he decided to enter the world of business. He had started in the Special Services of the Dutch army as a sergeant and was discharged with the rank of major with $18,000, some of which came to him in accumulated pay, as he never received more than a sergeant's wage. Using this money, and with additional funds from his family, in the summer of 1946 he bought a small restaurant equipment manufacturing company in Toronto from AGA Heat Canada Ltd. (the Canadian arm of a British manufacturer which produced heat storage stoves that were popular in Europe and Quebec). According to Robbert's recollection, AGA had started a distributorship in Canada before the war, around 1936. After the war broke out and the inventory of AGA cookers in Canada was sold, there was nothing left to sell. The manager in Canada started to make a few large kitchen products of sheet metal. When, in 1946, the British directors found out that they were responsible for a very small manufacturer, they decided to sell it. Robbert purchased the company in November 1946, and changed the company name to Kitchen Installations Ltd. With this, KIL was founded.

Fairfax Financial at the New York Stock Exchange. Robbert (fourth from the left) and Prem Watsa, founder, chairman, and CEO of Fairfax (fourth from the right).

Robbert started with four employees at the KIL Toronto premises on Bloor Street, close to Jane Street. One of those employees was Edward I. Blake, a young salesman inherited from the AGA Heat Canada Ltd. purchase. This was the beginning of Edward's long service to the company. The company produced stainless steel food service items and soon focused on designing and manufacturing stainless steel sinks. KIL grew quickly, and in the late 1940s Robbert sold the Toronto factory and rented space in Building 310, a former munitions filling factory in Ajax, Ontario. "As coal-fired household cookers (like AGA) were not easy to sell, we abandoned the distribution (and service!!) of AGA cookers in 1949 or 1950," Robbert recalled. Consumers began to recognize the advantages of stainless steel, namely its cleanliness and durability. Plumbers appreciated the excellent features developed by KIL. In Ajax the company met this demand with practical and innovative products, such as the self-rimming ledge, the Easy Clamp flexible ledge fastening system, the Spillway partition, and highly polished finishes.

Early photographs of the Kitchen Installations Ltd. factory.

In 1954 the company had become "Manufacturers of Metal Products — Fabricating — Spinning — Casting — Pressing — Equipment for Industrial, Hospital, Hotel, and Restaurant Use." Imagine the shining, stainless steel cafeterias and restaurant kitchens of the early 1950s, with their steam tables and gleaming cylindrical coffee urns — these are the types of products produced by KIL. In the early 1950s KIL marketed the Style Queen, a line of pots and pans made with stainless steel on the outside and with copper within for heat diffusion. The Style Queen logo was imprinted on the pieces with the taglines "Stainless Steel with a Heart of Copper" or "Stainless Steel Clad Copper." The brand name was a precursor to the Steel Queen — the company's flagship sink that was trademarked in 1954. Robbert capitalized on the growing market interest in stainless steel sinks, and KIL's strategy to promote the Steel Queen was to create a brand franchise with a loyal industry following. The Steel Queen sinks were reserved exclusively for sale by plumbers and marketed for their quick and easy installation.

In 1954 Robbert met Herb de Jong, a metallurgist who had also emigrated from The Netherlands with his family. Herb had been promised a job with Dofasco Steel Company in Hamilton, but when he arrived his employer was involved in a strike and his position was put on hold until the dispute was resolved. At this time, Robbert was looking for a new production manager and his cousin Huug van Dantzig in Holland mentioned Herb's qualifications and his recent arrival in the area. The two men met and Robbert immediately hired Herb as Production Manager for KIL — a position he held for the next 25 years. Robbert's father, Arthur (who was Chairman of the Board of Directors at the time), was not impressed with Robbert's decision. Upon hearing of Herb's hiring, Arthur said, "We have hired a very irresponsible young man — he came to Canada with his wife and five children and no money." Arthur was serious and Robbert was angered at his father's distrust of his decision. He said, "He's hired and that's it." Robbert and Herb went to the secretary and she wrote a check for two weeks salary advance for Herb, even though he had yet to see the factory. "That was Robbert," remarked Herb. If he wanted you and he knew you would fit the position, he made it happen.

Robbert had his own management style, as Herb, who was hired when he was 33 years old, recalls. Once Robbert found out that he could do the job, he left Herb alone: "Now what we did do, both being from Dutch heritage, we fought together, like we got mad at each other at times because Dutch people can do that pretty good and we would shout at each other in Dutch. We would never swear." Both men smoked cigars and, after a fight, Robbert would say, "Okay, that's enough," and they would have a cigar together. Robbert had a temper, and many who knew him saw a glimpse of this at one time or another. "He would put his hands in his pockets and he would start walking with small paces and then, you know, oh boy, there he comes, you better stay out of his way and that's how you knew he was angry," Herb recalled. "It would never last long. He was honest about it, he would never say, 'I'm right and you're wrong.' He wouldn't be like that."

Robbert hired Don Dowdell as Secretary-Treasurer in 1954. Don was the accountant who previously audited KIL's books and he continued as Secretary-Treasurer for the next 25 years. Don and Robbert also maintained a friendship for decades — even after their work at KIL, Robbert continued to hire Don to work with him on the Industrial Research and Development Institute in the 1990s. Don was also asked to be the power of attorney for Robbert, "because I was a friend." That meant a lot to him and he always appreciated Robbert's time and recognition of such milestones as Don's wedding anniversary. Although Don was Robbert's friend and employee for many years, he is still amazed by Robbert's scope of accomplishments. "There are many things that I didn't know about. He was involved in so many things."

Under Robbert's leadership, KIL continued to grow and thrive. In 1955 Robbert purchased an AGA Industries plant in Pembroke, Ontario. And KIL soon proclaimed itself "Canada's Largest Manufacturer of Stainless Steel Sinks." In 1959 the Steel Queen name was proudly electro-etched on every sink bowl. By the early 1960s, enamel sinks had almost disappeared from the Canadian market, as KIL products earned the respect of consumers and plumbers worldwide.

In the early 1960s, a militant labour environment developed in the Oshawa-Ajax area. According to Don, the KIL plant was near a General Motors factory and the workers sought to have their wages match what the neighbouring company was offering. Along with this demand, several incidents of vandalism convinced Robbert to look for a new community to sustain KIL's continued growth. Robbert also looked for opportunities to locate three plants outside of Canada. In an address to the Penetanguishene Lions Club in 1963 he explained the process: "At the outset the company set up a scoring system on six specifications laid down for municipalities they would consider. First they wanted a town of under 30,000 population with available labour, and a history of good labour relations. They needed good subsoil for heavy machinery, ten acres of serviced land close to main arteries." A map survey indicated 76 favourable municipalities. After applying the six requirements, the number was reduced to 26. KIL then conferred with its bankers to obtain more information, and four locations came out with the highest ratings. KIL gave consideration to municipalities with fire protection, police protection, banks, tool shops, and printing establishments. Robbert said KIL was "interested in housing, availability of schools and how good they were, churches, recreation and friendliness of the town ... All of these things I have enumerated were the factors that brought us to Midland." The company asked key personnel to look at these locales. The municipalities were questioned on the willingness and availability of labour; electric, gas, and water rates; economic-mindedness of the community; historical background of industry in the community; and tax rates. In his address to the Lions Club, Robbert exploded the notion that industries are lured to municipalities through tax concessions. Robbert insisted that this was not a factor. "We weren't interested, because when it comes down to the fine point someone has to pay and eventually we could be paying for another industry's tax holiday."

From the top four municipalities, Robbert decided to move KIL to Midland, Ontario. Robbert knew the Midland-Penetanguishene area and had moored his boat there for several years. In March 1962 KIL completed negotiations for the purchase of land on Highway 12, just inside the town's eastern boundary. The decision was confirmed when Robbert purchased a home in Midland on Hugel Avenue West. Construction began in the spring of 1962 on the new 40,000-square-foot KIL factory. In order to effectively describe the business, the company also changed its name from Kitchen Installations Ltd., to Kindred Industries Ltd. — strategically retaining the KIL initials. By the 1960s, KIL specialized in three fields — stainless steel sinks, restaurant pans, and ductless steel hoods. Robbert said, "Steel sinks made in the Midland plant will find their way into many countries, as well as all provinces of Canada. The company exports this product to South and Central America, Singapore and Manila, among other places."

At the end of July 1962, KIL closed its Ajax plant and the next week the Midland plant was completed and operations began. The new factory employed two shifts of workers, about 70 people, some 45 of whom received training in Penetanguishene at the former Breithaupt Leather tannery. The senior management of KIL, as well as a handful of other employees, followed KIL to Midland. The KIL Social Club, formed in 1962, helped smooth the transition for new employees. The Social Club held several dinner dances throughout the year, at Christmas, Valentine's Day and Halloween. The members paid dues to support club events such as a fishing derby, Western Night barbecue, three golf tournaments, various bus excursions and a Georgian Bay boat cruise. The club also arranged for ice time at a local rink for employee hockey Friday afternoons throughout the winter.

Kindred Industries Ltd. continued to grow, successfully merging with a series of other stainless steel sink producers. It became the holding company of an international group of companies specializing in the production of stainless steel sinks. In 1965 KIL merged with Arista Products Ltd., makers of stainless steel sinks, located in Toronto. That company joined the KIL international group of stainless steel sink manufacturing companies in Canada, Europe and the United States, with activities in 23 countries. Robbert also purchased a sink manufacturing factory owned by Zeigler Harris in Los Angeles, California, and in 1970 he opened a Zeigler Harris plant in Pinegrove, Pennsylvania. In the late 1960s, Herb and Robbert travelled to Belgium, The Netherlands, and Luxemburg (countries which were working on economic development at the time). According to Herb, Robbert bought some buildings in Rijssen, in eastern Holland, and developed a factory there under the name of Reginox N.V. Herb and Don were instrumental in setting up the systems within the factory, and frequently went back to observe the factory's progress. Robbert's brother-in-law Oliver Mansell (Ellen's husband) managed the new factory. In 1975 KIL sold Reginox N.V., but it remained one of the major sink makers in the Netherlands.

A multi-phase expansion of the KIL factory in Midland was announced in the spring of 1966. Robbert explained that the KIL board of directors decided to proceed with the extension, which would begin with a first phase that consisted of a 50 per cent increase in the existing factory space with an additional 19,000-square-foot extension to the south of the existing plant. This would accommodate a new product line and enable KIL to serve the increasing market in the United States, and to meet this demand the company announced an addition of approximately 25,000 square feet to its plant on what was renamed Kindred Road. The addition, completed in the summer of 1968, was designed for the manufacture of smaller items and was attached to the existing building. The plant now contained a total of 85,000 square feet.

As the company grew, so did the number of its employees. They adjusted well to life in Midland. As a boater, Robbert particularly enjoyed his new town near the shores of Georgian Bay, where he could dock his boat at a local marina. Robbert was always grateful for Midland's reception of KIL, and he continually showed his gratitude with respect for his employees and with his extensive charity work within the community. When KIL manufactured its one millionth sink in 1967, plant manager Herb de Jong presented it to J.A. Craig, administrator of St. Andrews Hospital in Midland. The administrator praised the part which Robbert and KIL played in furthering the welfare of the town during the comparatively short period the plant had been in operation.

The company flourished and in 1973 Robbert expanded the interests of KIL, amalgamating the two premier Canadian plumbing companies: Waltec Industries (owned by the Burgess family), of Wallaceburg, Ontario, and KIL. This created a major Canadian manufacturer that became

Waltec Enterprises Ltd. According to Jim Forgie (former Vice-President and General Manager of Waltec Forgings), the new company consisted of Kindred Industries, Reginox, and Arista (all companies Robbert owned), and Waltec Industries, which consisted of Wallaceburg Brass, Galt Brass, Wallaceburg Engineering, Wallaceburg Forgings (50 per cent owned by Delta Metals, a United Kingdom company in a joint venture), Aquarobic Home Sewage Treatment Systems, and Domidco Sales (all Burgess companies). For 14 years before the merger Robbert sat on the Wallaceburg board of directors, so he was familiar with the company. "I believe at the time of the merger Kindred had 60 per cent of the stainless steel sinkware market in Canada and Wallaceburg/Galt had 32 per cent of the two-handle faucet business in Canada," said Jim. "Wallaceburg Brass had just finished tooling new production lines to produce all the faucet needs for the total Canadian market (kitchen sink, lavatory basin, and tub and shower). Galt Brass had a low-cost green sand automated brass foundry."

Waltec Enterprises was valued at $14,100,000 at the time of the sale. Robbert maintained a 51 per cent controlling interest in the amalgamated company, with the Burgess family having 29 per cent, and a British company, Delta Metals, owning 20 per cent. With his majority interest, Robbert became President and Chief Executive Officer of Waltec Enterprises Ltd. and controlled a number of plumbing-related operations in Midland, Toronto, Cambridge, Wallaceburg and Cornwall, Ontario; and Kansas City, Missouri and Waterbury, Connecticut. Instead of centralizing with one management group, Waltec Enterprises Ltd. (Waltec) set up operating divisions to respond to market opportunities and demands quickly and with single-mindedness. In addition to produc-tion, engineering, and accounting, each division had its own marketing and sales group. Part of the restructuring included a corporate office in Cambridge, Ontario, to manage and offer guidance to the divisions.

In 1978 Robbert moved to Cambridge to run Waltec. He lived in a very modest home on Township Road 27A, near East Galt. Although Robbert spent much of his time in Cambridge over the next six years, he also maintained a residence in Perkinsfield, in Tiny Township, just outside of Midland. He purchased this house in Perkinsfield on a large property surrounded by lush trees in the spring of 1981. Robbert was also in Midland during his monthly visit to the company's operations there. Indeed, he visited each Waltec Enterprises operation monthly.

Robbert sought to better every community in which he lived and those where his employees lived and prospered. Even though Cambridge was his home for only a few years, Robbert became involved with the local YMCA, as well as Scouting in the area.

In 1975, Waltec Enterprises Ltd. acquired Eastern Pottery, which made toilets, in Cornwall, Ontario. This became Waltec Bathware. Under Robbert's direction, Waltec continued to flourish through the turn of the decade. In the late 1970s, a new generation of senior managers assumed responsibilities at Kindred Industries in Midland. Hudson Leavens, a young MBA and former Materials Manager at Kindred (also a former Scout of Robbert's), became Vice-President and General Manager. Hudson recalled that Robbert "was very, very clever when it came to manufacturing … He would know more about it than the engineers." Robbert and Hudson became good friends and he marveled at Robbert's worldliness, saying, "One of the things that fascinated me about Robbert was, if you had been somewhere obscure in the world, like Madagascar, you would mention it and tell a story about it and Robbert would correct you. He would tell you that you had the wrong street. He had been everywhere. He had an amazing brain that could retain everything about these places." David Webster (current CEO and CFO of Baytech Plastics and a former Scout of Robbert's) was hired in 1976 to work with Waltec to comply with the recently introduced Anti-Inflation Act. David became CEO of Waltec Plastics and worked closely with Robbert from 1982 to 1986. He remembered Robbert's impatience, recalling an incident when Robbert purchased a new company. Robbert told the lawyer, "I'm ready to sign. If it's not ready in half an hour I'm walking away."

"It was ready," said David. He also recalled one time at lunch with Robbert and when it was time to order, David was not quite ready and said he would have what Robbert ordered. It turned out to be his first tartare sandwich. David also reflected on Robbert's hands-on management approach. Robbert "didn't want the head office to be seen as an ivory tower — it was more of a service." He had great respect for the managers of the companies. He could leave the operations for weeks or months at a time because he trusted those in leadership positions within the company. Some of Robbert's employees, like Hudson and David, came to know him as a friend and maintained this relationship with him for decades.

Robbert treated all of his employees with respect. His friend Tom Gibson observed, "Robbert was pretty adept in terms of judging a person's capabilities, so he didn't lead you astray. He set you off on things he was comfortable that you could handle. He was very astute in that way. That was something he brought to his business life as well. The sense I had from his business activities was not only was it growing … but the people that

Robbert (left), Hudson Leavens
(centre), and Bobby Orr (right) at
a Waltec function.

worked for him were immensely loyal to him." This loyalty is evident in the
number of employees who worked for Waltec for decades.

Anton Mudde (president of Baytech Plastics in Midland) was also
impressed by Robbert's foresight to recognize that plastic was becoming
a large part of the plumbing industry in the 1980s. Anton appreciated
Robbert's vision of using the latest technology to lower production costs and
he thought that Robbert was "very progressive in what he was trying to do"
with the business in his "quietly demanding" way. "He stepped in at the right
times, did the right things, motivated a whole bunch of people … He always
had an opinion, again, never forcing things on people. That was his presence."

In a letter to Waltec Enterprises Ltd. directors in August 1982, Robbert
wrote, "Our motto remains: cut costs wherever possible, cut inventories,
maintain market share." He always insisted on looking at the "total Waltec"
picture. Waltec had sales of $86,070,000 and a profit of $4,626,000
in the year-end of 1983. By 1984 Waltec had ten plants employing 1,455
people. That same year, *Canadian Business* magazine listed Waltec among
its 25 most profitable businesses in the country, with $100 million in
annual sales. David said Robbert would have liked to have seen the

Two of Waltec's major product lines were faucets and custom components. Robbert addressing a crowd at a Waltec Faucets meeting.

company go public, but this never came to fruition, because the timing was not right. In the early 1980s Robbert began talking to Emco Ltd., Masco's Canadian company based in London, Ontario. Emco's 1983 annual report stated, "With manufacturing facilities in eight countries, Emco Limited is a worldwide leader in the manufacture and distribution of fluid handling products, from bathroom faucets to service station nozzles to marine arms used for the transfer of petroleum products to and from tankers."

In 1984 Robbert turned 65 years old and decided it was time to slow down, even if only a little. After what he called a "minor health scare," he decided to sell Waltec Enterprises for $38 million. In March 1984, negotiations were completed and for the first time, after operating as a private company since 1905, Waltec became associated with the many companies in the Masco Corporation of Taylor, Michigan. On June 15 at the law firm of Ivey and Dowler in the Northern Life Tower City Centre in London, Ontario, Emco Ltd. finalized the purchase of all shares of Waltec Enterprises, other than those owned by Delta Group Overseas Ltd. Robbert represented himself, Waltec Enterprises, and Waltec Inc. Jack Iles became president and CEO of Waltec, but Robbert stayed on as chairman of the board of directors. The company continued to make its line of products as a separate entity under existing management. In November 1984, Robbert wrote;

> In the last few months ... I have given a lot of thought as to how I can help make the transition in management of Waltec as smooth as possible. I am well aware of my aggressive tendencies (for which I do not apologize) and am very sensitive to the necessity of providing full freedom in all aspects for the "new" team ... It is, I believe, very useful if we can start this new phase for Waltec without retaining, perhaps unstated, obligations on the part of the new management towards me, nor any expectations on my part. I therefore enclose, as per January 1, 1985, my resignation. However, it would be completely wrong to draw the conclusion from this that I am anxious to sever all relationships or want to "walk away" from any involvement in the future. I am, as I stated in September, quite prepared to consider fulfilling duties that you ask me to fulfill and I feel capable of handling.

However, it appeared to me that it would be much easier for all concerned that we start with a blank piece of paper — so that you two can be absolutely free to approach me whenever you wish, and that you feel there are absolutely no obligations on your part to ask for anything. I am quite convinced that Waltec/Emco is in excellent hands and that it will prosper. I am also very satisfied in the way the succession has been handled.

As it turned out, Robbert remained a director of Emco for only a short time. Emco did not have the same mission and values as Waltec, and therefore, it was difficult for Robbert to watch decisions that did not favour former Waltec divisions. "He was protective and thought we should be supported in any project we could 'justify,'" David Webster noted. "Emco had a different way to evaluate and approve projects." Although Robbert was no longer directly involved in the company, he remained a constant source of advice and support for those employees with whom he had worked at Waltec. David Webster recalled, "During the time when senior management was integrating into Emco, Robbert was always available to coach or offer advice when requested. If he felt strongly, he would contact us and give suggestions …The Waltec Plastics Division (now Baytech Plastics Inc.) sent monthly financial statements to Robbert for some 15 years after his formal involvement ceased. He would usually send a letter of caution or congratulations every few months. He was still brilliant with numbers well into his 80s!" Anton also appreciated Robbert's continued involvement and encouragement. "He is a man you could respect, no matter what he was doing, whether you were doing the right things, wrong things, by the end of the day, he had great respect for what you were doing."

Upon the sale of Waltec in 1984, Jim Burgess wrote to Robbert saying, "You have established a challenging target for the future: to beat your own past performance." Robbert remained interested in the business of Waltec and KIL, as he continued as a mentor for many of his former employees. In the 1990s, when Walter Franke purchased KIL from Emco, Robbert noted, "Walter Franke began his successful corporation with catering equipment, not that different from KIL. I remember vividly my first visit to their immaculate Swiss factory. They have always been a first rate, honourable manufacturer of quality products, and are truly a class act. I believe that a Franke-Kindred combination (whatever the name will be, that is not too important) will be beneficial for both parties and, therefore, rejoice in its completion."

Throughout Robbert's business career and after his retirement (his activities after he sold Waltec can hardly be classified as a retirement), he was a director of a number of companies. According to his personal records, he was a director and member of the Audit Committee for Alis Technology Inc., Hugh Russel Inc., Atlantis International Resources Ltd., Russel Metals Inc., Fairfax Financial Holdings Ltd. and Morden Helwig Ltd. He was also a director of Dalex Co. Ltd., Hughes-Leitz Optical Technology Ltd., Padinox Ltd. (commonly known as Paderno), Emco Ltd., Markle Community Newspapers Ltd., Municipal Financial Co. Ltd., Foreign Investment Trust Inc., Bayweb Ltd., Wallaceburg Brass Ltd., and Insurance Company of Evanston Inc. He was also a shareholder in several of the companies. Three companies that he served for a number of years include Paderno, Fairfax Financial Holdings, and Russel Metals.

COMPANY RELATIONSHIPS
Paderno Inc.

George Serra, formerly of Milan, Italy, formed Paderno in December 1977 when he and his wife emigrated to Canada to avoid problems facing industrialists in the north of Italy and started in Prince Edward Island (PEI). Their goal was to make long-lasting cookware. Robbert became involved with Paderno in April 1981, when he wrote to the chairman of Paderno, Warren Hurst, saying, "As my technical interests are directly related to deep drawing of stainless steel, and moreover as I started my business career, coming back from my army service overseas, by making pots and pans (in cast aluminum), I have had a special interest (and perhaps some inside knowledge) in this Paderno venture." Later that month Warren invited Robbert to be a board member for Paderno, confiding, "I believe it very important for George Serra to have successful people with experience in allied fields not only available for him to consult but also as board members to set priorities and policies." In June 1981, Robbert, Herb deJong, and Bill Storey (a friend of Robbert's) travelled to Charlottetown to analyze the Paderno plant, and from this trip, Robbert wrote Warren, saying, "I am prepared to give you my support as indicated earlier, mostly because I have confidence in you and the group — a little less because I like the products and very little because I like the factory set-up (except for very good equipment and dies). Please remember that I am only interested if all the required capital is raised and only if a sufficiently strong and knowledgeable board is created." Thus began Robbert's more than 25 years of service to Paderno.

Paderno was a growing company and it had its troubles over the years. Robbert was always persistent in keeping it accountable and efficient. After receiving a late financial statement he quipped, "To get Paderno under control, monthly figures by the end of the fifth working day after month end should be a real target!!!!" Poor sales resulted in financial problems. According to Jim Casey (chairman of the board), Robbert supported the company during this time by proposing reorganization and by contributing extra funds that allowed the company to continue in business. In 1982, when Jim became involved with Paderno, Robbert was chairman of the board of directors. That year, Robbert wrote, "The company is not doing well (that is the understatement of the century)." Robbert invested more money in the company when Paderno was struggling, as did Jim, and soon its finances turned around. "Robbert was a very unselfish person," said Jim. "Robbert always offered advice … He would always study his board material before meetings … He was always out to see the company succeed — it was a challenge for him … He wanted to succeed and that was more important than anything else." Robbert's greatest satisfaction was to make things work. Robbert's broad, contextual thinking, as well as his attention to detail, made him a valuable asset to Paderno's board. He often read, digested, and reread company reports. He said he needed 7 to 12 hours to get fully through most reports.

The Paderno board meetings were held in Charlottetown, and some in Toronto. Robbert frequently flew to PEI to attend the meetings. Jim recalled, too, that Robbert could not wait to get to the island to have some good lobster.

By 1985, Paderno began to succeed. "We are approaching 1985 with a strong sense of hard-won confidence about our future," a company write-up boasted. "This self-confidence is in no way to be misconstrued as 'cockiness.' It is deeper than that and is a reflection of the fact that in 1984 we steered our way around and through imminent corporate disaster. Further, it is a recognition that all of the participants in our company, employees, management, and shareholders, all played separate but significant roles in the survival of Paderno Inc." Sales started to climb and continued to do so into the 1990s. Robbert joked to Jim in 1994, "Wednesday at a directors' meeting I was asked by one of the gentlemen present if I could use my influence to ban future 'factory sales of Paderno cookware' in Midland. Last year the gentleman's wife bought six pans and this year four more and he knows she will buy some more next time, so could I stop this expenditure? I stated that definitely I would NOT accommodate him. It shows very nicely that one sale leads to better things for the next one." (Robbert personally supported the company's products when in November 1984 he ordered a Paderno cookset and in January 1995 a Chandier frypan.)

In the late 1990s Robbert and Jim began talking about Robbert selling his Paderno shares to the Casey family. "As promised I gave thought to the sale of shares," Robbert wrote in October 1998. "If I had my druthers I would keep the shares as — thanks to you — the company is in excellent shape, and bound to go ahead in the next few years. However, I also realize that holding on to these shares may provide difficulties if you would have to deal with a stranger and that would be unfair to the Casey family." He offered to sell his shares and said, "Whatever your decision is, I would greatly enjoy contributing as a (too vocal — but vitally interested) director of Padinox, as it is great fun to be associated with a progressive company that has a tremendous future." Jim respected Robbert's offer and appreciated his fairness. He purchased 50 per cent of the shares of Paderno and took control of the company. Robbert made this arrangement possible because he sold his shares at a reasonable and fair price, as he was more concerned with the overall success of the company than with personal gain. "He was always out for your best interests," said Jim.

Paderno began as manufacturers of cookware and sold their products to retail stores. With the growing success of the company, Paderno started to open its own stores and factory outlets and began adding products other than cookware. Now 50 to 60 per cent of their sales are not in cookware and Paderno has become a wholesaler, as well as a manufacturer.

Robbert attempted to resign from Paderno on a couple of occasions — once to ease the transition for the Caseys so that they would not have to deal with an outside director. In July 2006 he wrote Jim saying, "If I insisted on getting another, younger director, it is not because I want to resign — but at my age those decisions are decided for me — and I would want to avoid any hiatus in governance." However, Robbert's records indicate a trip to Charlottetown in February 2007 for a board meeting, so he did stick around.

Robbert was optimistic about Paderno's progress, saying, "The future (always somewhat unknown and, therefore, threatening) appears bright — real fun!!" Robbert respected Jim Casey and thoroughly enjoyed his journey with Paderno. Jim said that it was through Paderno that Robbert was introduced to a very valuable business contact — John Watson at Confederation Life Insurance Co. When Robbert asked John whom he would recommend to him to manage his money, John recommended his former employee, a Mr. Prem Watsa.

Fairfax Financial Holdings

In 1984 Prem Watsa, commonly referred to as Canada's Warren Buffet, founded a company with Tony Hamblin called Hamblin Watsa Investment Counsel, a money management company. Robbert was one of his first clients. After he sold Waltec, Robbert wanted someone to manage his growing pool of money. Shortly after Prem started Hamblin Watsa, Robbert sent him a cheque in the mail for approximately one million dollars. "My secretary almost fell off her chair when she got the cheque," Prem recalled. "So we began. I got to know Robbert and I got this idea." A small company in Toronto was going through some problems, so I said to Robbert, "I think there's an opportunity here, I want to talk to you about it. I'll have breakfast with you." Robbert had been his client for less than a year. Prem presented his idea to take over a small Toronto-based insurance company. Robbert simply said, "How much do you need?" Prem replied, "$400,000." "You've got it." Prem still had to show Robbert all of the numbers, but Robbert insisted he was behind him. "So that's how I met Robbert Hartog," Prem said in an amused kind of way.

This small insurance company became Fairfax Financial Holdings. Over the next 23 years, Robbert was on the board of directors and on a number of committees, including the Charitable Donations Committee; he was Chairman of the Audit Committee, and Prem's key confidant. The stock price of Fairfax rose from $3.25 in 1985 to $350 in 2008. Prem said there were a core group of investors from the beginning and some sold shares at different times, but Robbert never sold a single share. His patience was rewarded and he remarked to Prem that he made more money with Fairfax than he made from his own company, which was undoubtedly the case when you multiply his early investments accordingly.

When Prem started Fairfax, a worldwide property casualty insurance and reinsurance company, he was only 35 years old, and he greatly valued Robbert's experience. Before becoming the founder, chairman, and CEO of Fairfax, Prem had immigrated to Canada from India in 1972 with little money and no contacts. He and Robbert were both immigrants; however, they both believed it was important to stay in Canada and pay taxes. Robbert simply said, "I came from Holland and I did very well. I made my money here, I pay my taxes here." In 1985 Prem put a group together and they took control of the small company that became Fairfax. "Robbert was there right through," said Prem. "Robbert was there with everything we did."

One of the guiding principles of Fairfax is, "Honest and integrity are essential in all our relationships and will never be compromised."

Robbert and Prem (fifth and fourth from the right respectively) at a Fairfax Financial gathering.

Robbert exuded integrity in all that he did. "He was a very successful businessman, extremely successful, and he had tons of integrity… He loved his work," commented Prem. At 87 years of age, Robbert told Prem, "I love this, I love this job." He said his dream was to pass away doing what he loved. It was rare to have an 87-year-old on a board of directors, but Robbert was still extremely sharp in the boardroom. (According to the New York Stock Exchange that year, there was only one man older than Robbert who was the chair of an Audit Committee.) At every milestone birthday, Prem would thank Robbert for his service in the company's annual report. On Robbert's 75th birthday, Prem remarked, "He has more energy than all of us combined and he keeps us on our toes." Robbert remained on the board until 2007, when he decided to scale back his activities because his health could not tolerate the travelling involved.

As a member of Fairfax's board of directors from 1985 to 2007, Robbert was a constant source of information and support for Prem, who praised Robbert: "Totally selfless, dependable, loyal, all the great qualities in life that you can have, Robbert had." Robbert was always very honest. He once asked Prem why he would want someone on his board who would point out things Prem was doing wrong. Prem replied, "That's why I want you on my board, because you're the only one that will tell me."

Prem explained that Robbert's approach to business was very simple. "He figured that you need to treat your customers well; treat your employees well; always excel in treating your employees and your customers well. Then ultimately you make money for your shareholders ... Do things right. It might cost you, but do it right. Do it right the first time." Robbert pushed the members of the Fairfax board to achieve excellence. "When he chaired a meeting, everyone knew he was chair. He would run the meeting, which he positively started on time. If he was not the chair, he would listen, but when he had a point to make, everyone would take note. He would often spend 20 hours on a weekend preparing for a board meeting, and because of this background knowledge," Prem said, "he knew our company better than anyone else."

Prem and Robbert had a special relationship. They were very involved in business, but also socially. Prem said he considered Robbert his "godfather." He had a great deal of respect for Robbert both, as a friend and as a businessman. Robbert kept a number of invitations to the annual

Robbert with Fairfax staff (third from the right, top row) and Prem (second from the left, top row).

Watsa Christmas party, which he regularly attended, as well as to annual meetings in Toronto or in various locations around the world. Tony Griffiths (whom Robbert knew from Russel Metals and who also sat on the Fairfax board of directors) said, "I think Fairfax was a priority for him because he was an original investor, an original director, had all these involvements on committees … He took it very seriously. It was a rare time when he wasn't physically there."

Prem and Robbert also travelled frequently on Fairfax business, to such places as Saskatoon, Vancouver, Paris, London, the Bahamas, and Barbados. While travelling, Robbert never had a problem with the time difference. He would have a two-to three-hour nap and then be ready to go. After a nap, he said to Prem, "I got more sleep than I usually get!" Fairfax bought a company in Chicago, so Prem and Robbert went there many times together. The owner of the business wanted to impress them, so he sent a stretch limousine to pick them up. Robbert hated this and refused to ride in it, but Prem convinced him for a couple of rides. After that, Prem advised the man not to send a limousine again. Robbert was never one for flashy parades of wealth or power.

All of the senior executives at Fairfax received a plaque that says, "There's no limit to what a man can do or where he can go if he doesn't mind who gets the credit" — a quotation attributed to Ronald Reagan. Prem ran Fairfax this way and Robbert embodied it. He did not care about credit; he just wanted to give back. A Fairfax trader once asked Robbert why he participated in Canadian Executive Service Organization — an organization that sends Canadian volunteers to various countries to help

Robbert donning his four-star general hat presented to him by Fairfax Financial.

Robbert (right) playing the slot machine on a trip with Prem (left).

businesses. The volunteers do not get luxurious accommodations and are often sent to developing nations. Robbert simply replied, "I really think I'm blessed, so I'm doing this to return what I've been given."

Russel Metals

Russel Metals, a Mississauga, Ontario-based metals distribution and trading business, is one of the largest steel distribution companies in North America. It also exports steel products to international end-users and imports foreign steel products into Canada and the United States. Robbert served on its board of directors from 1997 to 2007 and was a member of the Audit Committee. Brian Hedges (current CEO and president of Russel Metals) said that Prem Watsa (founder, chairman, and CEO of Fairfax Financial Holdings), an investor in Russel Metals, nominated Robbert to the board in 1997. According to the company's 1997 Operational Review, "The directors bring to the company a balance of industry and operational expertise as well as backgrounds in other areas which the board believes are of benefit … The board's mandate is to supervise the management of the business and affairs of the company."

Robbert was a strategic person to have as a member of any board. His knowledge and experience made him a very valuable asset. Bud Siegel (former President and CEO of Russel Metals) said, "He was always there when we needed him." The board meetings were usually held in Toronto and Mississauga. During the meetings, Robbert "was a champion about issues that he was concerned about, he was a mentor for management

Robbert was impressed with the tremendous business success Russel Metals achieved during his ten years as a member of the Board of Directors.

figures … He was a very analytical thinker and was very, very supportive of management if he felt that management was setting a course that he was comfortable with," Bud explained. "He certainly was not afraid to advise management when he disagreed; he is what you always look for in a director."

Robbert was forward-thinking and notified management of upcoming issues or business trends. In May 2000 he wrote Bud saying, "I thought I should alert you that (and it could be 3 to 5 years hence) the use of aluminum tube for hydroforming automotive parts could be very substantial. This is simply an advance warning." The Honourable Mr. Justice Martin H. Freedman, who was on the board with Robbert, wrote to him in August 2002, saying, "If all board members on public companies had your insight, knowledge and tenacity, the marketplace and the companies inhabiting it would be all sound and credible."

Brian Hedges explained about working with Robbert that, "There was a dialogue with him, probably more than with any other director … He had a feel for business, had a good feel for capital markets. He understood the role of director, not to run the company, but to help us."

Robbert nominated Tony Griffiths as chairman of the Board, and the two worked together on the Russel Metals board from 1997. They also worked together on the Fairfax Financial Holdings board. Tony recalled that Robbert was "always the elder statesman … He was always the man of experience." Although he was a man of few words, Robbert was "abrupt but not confrontational", he did not suffer fools lightly, and he had a dry sense of humour. He described Robbert as "very perceptive, very direct, and I would classify him as being very proactive. He wasn't hanging around waiting for things that he wasn't hearing or finding information about something. He would get right into it, he wouldn't hesitate. People universally respected him because of his appearance and his forthrightness." Tony reflected, "If I had to list the three best directors I have ever known, he is certainly one of the three."

Tony was undoubtedly saddened in November 2006 when Robbert wrote to inform him, "The excellent trip to Edmonton convinced me that physically I find it very difficult to travel. Therefore, I request that I do not be named as a director, at the next AGM of Russel. I have greatly enjoyed the openness of the meetings and it is with deep regret that I write this letter. I would like to thank you, Bud, Brian and many others for all the courtesies extended to me. The Russel story of the last 9 to 10 years is one that should be written up, as it is a story of revival, with tremendous success, of a corporation. I will have the opportunity to speak to my fellow directors at the upcoming meetings, but I felt I should let you know, at once, about my decision. It has been most pleasant to work with you over these years." Tony took Robbert's request to the other directors, but they all wanted Robbert to stay on the board. Although Robbert travelled to Fort Myers, Florida, on Russel Metals business in February 2007, his term on the board ended that year.

CHAPTER THREE

Innovation in Education

All his life Robbert Hartog valued education and innovation. In his business life he strove for excellence and improvement and this flowed over to his philanthropic endeavours. From his interests and experience in manufacturing, Robbert especially supported education in engineering. Although he was trained as an economist, engineering was at the heart of his business. To ensure quality education for future generations, Robbert supported Georgian College, the University of Waterloo, and the University of Toronto — each renowned for engineering programs or apprenticeships. He saw the value in lessons on theory in a classroom, but Robbert emphasized practical skills to fuel research for industries. He especially saw a need for more practical research in the tool, die, and mould industries and he wanted to base this research in Midland. This culminated in an initiative in which Robbert and Reinhart Weber founded the Industrial Research and Development Institute (IRDI) in 1992. IRDI's goal was to be the leading self-supporting supplier of research and technical information to the tool, die and mould industries and its customers, as well as to educational institutions (namely the University of Waterloo and the University of Toronto) and government. In the long run, the IRDI would also play a critical role in the development of programs at Georgian College.

The opening of the Industrial Research and Development Institute in Midland. Witnessing the ribbon cutting ceremony is Robbert (far right), Paul Martin (second to the right) and Colin Harper (fourth from the right).

Industrial Research and Development Institute

In the late 1980s Reinhart Weber came to Robbert with the idea of building a training centre for the tooling industry in the area. He recognized the shortage of skilled people in industry, so Reinhart called Robbert to his office to speak with him about the idea, and they agreed that such a project was necessary. A steering committee was set up, including Bill Lennox, former dean of engineering at the University of Waterloo, Ron Venter, former chair and vice-Dean of Applied Sciences and Engineering at the University of Toronto, Don Dowdell, Robbert, and Reinhart. "It was one of the most difficult projects that Robbert and I ever took on," said Reinhart. This was because the government did not want to support IRDI, as it was not a university or a college, but an organization created for industry; therefore, funding was difficult to get. "There was never enough funding," said Reinhart.

In the early 1990s, facing severe financial cuts, including grants to universities, the government eliminated all funding to research organizations except universities. When IRDI was originally approved it was under a two-year funding agreement and the hope was that the funding would continue, but it did not. "So we had a real struggle for a period of time and that was when Robbert stepped in and donated money at various times to keep IRDI afloat." According to Reinhart, Robbert personally supported IRDI with loans that were turned into donations. If a deficit situation arose with an organization in which Robbert believed, he would financially assist.

The official offer from the Government of Ontario for IRDI funding had begun in the fall of 1991 and IRDI was founded in 1992 to accelerate the development of advanced technologies in industry. Robbert was chairman of the board of directors and Reinhart was vice-chairman. The board first met on January 20, 1992, in the Fairfax boardroom in Toronto. The concept was that the Institute would have a close relationship with the universities and also with industry. According to its promotional material, IRDI was a not-for-profit partner of innovative companies committed to excellence in parts design and manufacturing. It was a private, member-driven organization that customized its engineering and development to provide the optimum solutions for challenges ranging from research to parts production.

The philosophy behind IRDI was explained by Colin Harper, former president and CEO of IRDI:

> Most other countries have large technical institutes, Germany being the prime example ... They basically bridge the technical research and industry. The concept is that the university comes up with an idea

and gets it to the stage where you can describe the concept, something like machining metal at high speed, then you need large industrial equipment and a sort of prototype manufacturing process to get it to the next stage. In a lot of countries there are these technical institutes that are partially funded by government, partially funded by industry, and also often have large foundations, and they help industry adopt new technologies. The idea was that IRDI was to establish the same thing in Canada.

Reinhart Weber, Robbert, and Colin Harper.

Both Robbert and Reinhart had European backgrounds and Reinhart had done some work with European institutes, so he was aware of the benefits. There was a need to do something in Midland in the late 1980s and early 1990s after the Mitsubishi plant closed, and IRDI was one of the ideas brought forward to generate employment. In a statement Colin gave to Paul Martin (at the time Canada's Minister of Finance) he pointed out, "If we had the same number of technical institutes as Germany, related to the size of our industry, we would have one every 75 kilometers between Windsor and Quebec City."

In June 1995 the IRDI facility officially opened on 649 Prospect Boulevard, Midland. "A very economical, yet very good-looking building, thanks to Human Resources Canada, now exists and it will be 'stocked' with $40 million worth of borrowed equipment incorporating the latest technology," Robbert wrote to Canadian Prime Minster Jean Chrétien in December 1994. With 55,000 square feet and 45 employees, IRDI opened to provide advanced technical, training, and research support to companies involved in shaping materials. This encompassed tool, die, mould, and related industries in Canada. There were materials testing laboratory facilities onsite, which provided member and non-member companies with a full range of services in plastics and composites, ceramics, and metal analysis. IRDI was specifically for the shaping of material, so it was mostly mechanical engineering and lubrication. "For shaping steel, the lubricant that's used when you shape it is very critical, and we actually probably became the leader of that in North America," recalled Colin Harper. IRDI's role was to facilitate research in organizations that were not large enough to have their own research and development departments and to assist the commercialization of research carried out by universities and government research and development organizations. IRDI was a Certified Education Center of the Fabricators and Manufacturers Association, International. To promote IRDI's commitment to education, the institute held several workshop series for industry, such as "Introduction of Prototyping for Plastic Parts," "Laser Machining for Manufacturing," and "Aspects of Stamping with Aluminum." Workshops were offered in Midland, and at the University of Windsor, or they could be presented at an industry's chosen site and tailored to members of a specific organization. Many well-known companies participated in workshops, including 3M Canada, Boeing Toronto, General Motors of Canada Ltd., IMAX Corporation, Research in Motion, Samsonite Canada Ltd., as well as Kindred Industries, Waltec Engineering, and Waltec Plastics. As the only research facility of its kind in Canada, the IRDI facility was equipped with production-scale equipment in metalforming, machining, and injection molding, and the institute proved its research capabilities in these areas.

While working on IRDI, Robbert's varied experiences came together — some techniques learned during his military days, some experiences from volunteer youth leader activities — from sitting as a member on committees to industrial experience. "It is nice to know that sometimes, accumulated and diversified experiences can be used and useful," wrote Robbert in 1991.

"Robbert's a really hands-off kind of guy... So as long as things were going well, he didn't get involved," said Colin. Meetings were held quarterly, and a general meeting held each year. On the board there were typically three representatives from the universities, five or six from industry, and a couple of people from the government that sat in on the meetings but did not vote. Robbert believed that IRDI had to be controlled by industry and for industry. Over 50 per cent of the revenue came from U.S. auto and steel industries. Also, the initiative had close ties with the Fraunhofer Institute in Germany. IRDI was member driven and in 2000 there were approximately 200 members. People on the payroll were almost all university graduates (about half had master's degrees and typically four to eight, PhDs). Both the University of Toronto and the University of Waterloo were involved early in IRDI's conception, and the institute was also associated with McMaster University for a time. The attraction for the universities was that IRDI had outlets to industry. The universities used the facilities and did research; sometimes they paid for the equipment through funding from the university.

Bill Lennox from the University of Waterloo had previously been part of the Province of Ontario's Robotics and Manufacturing initiative, which ultimately became the Ontario Centre for Manufacturing Research. The University of Waterloo was a major player — along with the University of

Robbert (near centre), Reinhart (second from the right), and Colin Harper (left from centre) at an IRDI gathering.

Toronto and McMaster University. This project was linked to a number of industries (auto, tool and die, manufacturing). Robbert and Reinhart were aware of the project, but they were concerned that there was not enough focus on the problems associated with tool and die industries. Bill Lennox presumed that they chose him for IRDI because of this background. Similarly, Reinhart and Robbert asked Ron Venter from the University of Toronto to join them in their attempt to prod IRDI to develop "a research training capability in Midland." Waterloo and Toronto were thus involved in the pre-meetings for IRDI from the beginning. Robbert wrote Ron in 2001, saying, "You and Bill Lennox encouraged the collaboration between universities and IRDI, a collaboration that — on both sides — was, and still is not fully understood, or properly implemented. Much still remains to be done, but you initiated the work."

"Robbert was very keen to actually get things moving. I was always impressed by his ability to take an idea and sort of keep plugging away at it, but in a creative way," said Ron. The relationship between IRDI and the universities was highly successful. As of 1998, more than 30 students at the University of Toronto benefited from the growing partnership. A non-exclusive alliance between IRDI and the University of Toronto contributed millions of dollars to the University of Toronto Foundation for sponsoring shared equipment and post-graduate research scholarships at IRDI. In this program, postgraduate students receive their education at the University of Toronto and they perform their research project(s) using the advanced industrial equipment, computers, and software available at IRDI.

At Waterloo, Bill Lennox and Professor of Engineering Roy Pick, facilitated a relationship between Robbert and the University. At first Bill's participation was the only Waterloo involvement with IRDI, but he soon became a member of the board and researchers from the university became involved with IRDI. Robbert was aware of Waterloo's and Toronto's excellent reputations in engineering, which is likely why he sought their involvement. Robbert wrote Roy Pick in 1997 saying, "The past and now enhanced collaboration between your University and IRDI has always been a major goal." According to Pearl Sullivan, Department chair of Mechanical and Mechatronics Engineering, Robbert came to Waterloo because the engineering department's research orientation was industrially focused. She believed that Waterloo was a good investment for the improvement of technology for industry. In 1997, Robbert pledged a gift towards the Robbert Hartog Graduate Scholarship program. Two or more scholarships are awarded annually to full-time University of Waterloo graduate students in the Faculty of Engineering conducting research in materials or material shaping in the Department of Mechanical Engineering, who hold an Ontario Graduate Scholarship or an Ontario Graduate Scholarship in Science and Technology. Adel Sedra, Dean of Engineering at The University of Waterloo, said that Robbert would come and meet with the award winners. "He always enjoyed meeting the students that he supported … and always talked about ideas for research. One of his research ideas was pursued in mechanical engineering for research."

David Johnston, the President of The University of Waterloo, first met Robbert in 1978 when they sat on the Emco board together. David had an enormous amount of respect for Robbert: "He was among the top ten business people that I have ever met because he was wise … He was very disciplined." "Robbert was focused on very essential things — work honestly, work hard, work smart, and get the job done," David reported. Robbert came to Waterloo to meet with the president and the Dean of Engineering on several occasions. They shared with him their plans and ambitions and they asked for his advice and his help. This led to his continued interest and support of the department. When David Johnston went to Midland to make a proposal for a large gift from Robbert for a new building for engineering, Robbert told him that he was not interested in having his name attached (which was a possibility offered to him), but he informed David that there would be money left to the university in his estate. David replied, "Don't leave your good money to me — give me some direction now." Robbert had enough faith in Waterloo that they would do the right thing with the gift.

In 2000, Robbert and Colin met with Paul Martin, who was Finance Minister at the time, and he arranged to put IRDI in the federal budget.

David Johnston, President of the University of Waterloo

That year, Paul Martin wrote Robbert, saying, "I know this has been a dream and your vision you had many years ago and I'm delighted that it has become a reality for you." In August 2000, John Manley, the federal Minister of Industry, announced $3 million of ministry support for IRDI's technology innovation and commercialization program for small and medium-sized enterprises.

IRDI and Georgian College: A Unique Precedent

IRDI needed more funds than the government was able to offer, so Robbert made several loans (that turned into donations) to IRDI over the next few years. When the money from the government started to dry up, it became obvious that there was not going to be any additional funding from that source. For years, individual donors financially supported IRDI, but the lack of federal and provincial government support was disappointing. Robbert was often frustrated when dealing with government bureaucracy. "Where there was government involvement, he always wanted to do something different from the bureaucrats. One of his objectives in life was to trump the bureaucrats and always do a better job than they could," said Colin Harper. "If he could not achieve what he wanted, then he would put his own money behind it and then try to leverage it to try and get what he wanted … Robbert always liked being the non-visible party." He was a strong influence behind politicians, but this was not apparent. According to Doug Lewis (former Member of Parliament for Simcoe North), Robbert did what he could with any Liberals who wondered why they should put money into IRDI.

Robbert's frustration with bureaucracy and its dealings with IRDI was one of the reasons that Colin and Robbert drove thousands of kilometres to do a tour of various universities and community colleges to ensure a strong future for the institute. Beyond the continued high-level research at the Universities of Waterloo and Toronto, the best local arrangement seemed to be with Georgian College.

Georgian College had been established as part of the formation of Ontario's community college system in 1967 to offer a wide range of learning opportunities, including academic upgrading, college preparation, apprenticeship, certificate, diploma, graduate certificate, college degree, and degree programs. With several campuses, including locations in Collingwood, Orangeville, and main campuses in Barrie, Orillia, and Owen Sound, Georgian College's programs included business/management studies, community studies, design and visual arts, engineering technology, health sciences, degree studies (including automotive management), and graduate studies.

It is no surprise that Robbert Hartog supported Georgian's emphasis on work experience and the college's focus on the automotive sector and engineering. He served on the Board of Governors for five years from 1975 to 1980. During that time he was also Chairman of the Audit Committee, and a member of the Finance, Property, and Administration Committee. Fellow board member and friend Arch Brown said that Robbert had a reputation for not just talking about things; he followed through and did them and he confided that Robbert always humbled him. In 1982 Robbert was a panel speaker at a workshop titled "College's Future Planning Workshop." Through his considerable contacts and influence, he helped to champion the establishment of the Centre for Automotive Parts and Expertise (CAPE) at the college's Barrie campus.

Robbert's contribution to the success of Georgian College was publically recognized on October 2, 2003, when Robbert was bestowed the honour of being made a Georgian Fellow. He was only the tenth individual since 1967 to be invested into the Fellowship of Georgian College. The honour recognized his lifetime achievement and outstanding support of higher education and lifelong learning. The Fellowship implies privileged membership and lifetime association with Georgian College. In 2004 the Robbert Hartog Scholarship for Excellence was founded to assist students who demonstrated academic merit, leadership qualities and financial need. The funds to support the award were received through Fairfax Financial Holdings Ltd. from 2004 to 2007and then the Sixty Three Foundation (the charitable arm of Fairfax) in 2008 on a yearly basis. The award is presented to a student who has demonstrated academic merit in their studies, excellent leadership and a clear financial need (the heaviest criterion being the latter). Robbert selected the recipient of the award after reviewing ten or so pre-selected applicants for review. In 2004 he was given ten of 44 applicants to review. The recipient in 2004, Kathleen Atchison, wrote Robbert in appreciation for the award: "I am writing this letter to thank you for your immense kindness towards us students ... You must have a place in your heart for college and university students in order to make this great sacrifice on your part. Your unselfishness has touched my heart." Brian Tamblyn, president of Georgian College, wrote Robbert in 2004, also in appreciation for his contribution: "The fact that you chose Georgian over many other deserving colleges and universities is just another example of why the College has been very privileged to have you as a partner and great friend for so many years."

Brian first met Robbert in 1985, but he got to know Robbert best during his nearly decade-long presidency at Georgian. He thought of Robbert as a father figure who always had time and advice. Brian said Robbert believed strongly in educating youth. This was paired with his interest in manufacturing: a skilled workforce was essential. Robbert and Brian met regularly to discuss issues. Robbert also attended the annual board meetings at the college, where he offered advice on matters such as the economy and politics. Brenda Webb, Brian's assistant, appreciated Robbert's approachability. For all of his accomplishments and worldliness, he was easy to talk to and down-to-earth.

In 2002 Colin Harper, Reinhart Weber, Robbert and Brian Tamblyn began preliminary discussions concerning aligning IRDI with a compatible, strong principal entity that could provide a stronger platform for IRDI. Robbert and Reinhart expressed their opinion that the simplest possible solution would be the best: transferring IRDI to Georgian College. "The operation was so small at that time that it didn't make much sense to continue. The building was the perfect site for Georgian College to expand into the Midland area. It's being used now better than ever before," said Reinhart. On March 25, 2003, Robbert presented a motion at the board of directors "that IRDI merge with Georgian College and the Corporation of IRDI be dissolved in accordance with the tabled resolution, as prescribed in IRDI's letters patent." The board unanimously approved the motion. On July 1, 2004, IRDI and Georgian College amalgamated.

Robbert remained involved with IRDI. In September 2003 Brian asked him to be a member of the IRDI Advisory Committee, an invitation Robbert graciously accepted. The amalgamation allowed IRDI to expand its capabilities in research and development by using Georgian's faculty and staff as resources, and increased its ability to apply for funding for which IRDI had not previously qualified. The original purpose of IRDI remained, but Georgian focused more on skilled trades and less on research with industry. IRDI was transformed into the new Midland campus for Georgian. On March 7, 2005, Georgian College officially opened the Midland Skilled Trades Centre, which was to become the leading facility of its kind in central Ontario for research and innovation. According to Brian Tamblyn, Robbert's passion for both Georgian and IRDI was instrumental in the two organizations signing a strategic merger agreement that generated immense benefits for students as well as businesses in Simcoe County and across Canada. One more of Robbert Hartog's passions had become successful, leaving an enduring legacy for future generations.

CHAPTER FOUR

Robbert and His Communities

R obbert Hartog first became involved with the YMCA as a young man in France in the 1930s. At the age of 12, Robbert and his brother Dolf started going to the YMCA in Versailles. "I have wonderful memories of my time there — the people I met and the friends I made," attested Robbert. When he moved to Midland in the early 1960s he rekindled his relationship with the YMCA. For over 40 years Robbert was active with the YMCA in that community, and then in Cambridge, and also on a national level and international levels with YMCA Canada and with the World Alliance of YMCAs. Over the years he also anonymously supported Y programs in Moose Factory and Sudbury, Ontario, to assist friends in those regions. He provided financial support for various fundraising endeavours and was also often at the helm of such drives. Robbert's involvement, or reinvolvement since his youth participation, began when he was invited to speak at a Y Men's dinner, shortly after he moved to Midland. By 1963 he became a volunteer on the board of directors. Such involvement would repeat itself throughout his career with the organization, as Robbert found himself working with the YMCA in various capacities over the years. Robbert appreciated the values of the YMCA and he worked to maintain this for generations to come.

Robbert recognized the positive impact of the YMCA in communities and he worked to provide facilities and activities for current and future generations to enjoy.

In 1963 the purpose of the Y was "A Worldwide Fellowship of Persons United by a Common Loyalty to Jesus Christ for the Purpose of Developing Christian Personality and a Christian Society." Although the wording changed over the years, the YMCA remained a place to meet friends, to participate in recreational activities, to develop leadership, to strive for physical fitness, and to experience personal growth. In 1963, the YMCA facility in Midland offered activities including basketball, dance lessons, a stamp club, paddle tennis, and recorder music. That year the Y rendered services to 1,500 youth, 200 men, and 150 women, who took part in various programs. As well, service organizations hosted meetings in the facilities. "What this has meant to the community is easily understood. It is obvious that this kind of work must continue," Robbert wrote in 1963 in a letter titled "Why give to the Y." Robbert supported the YMCA because it encouraged the development of healthy people and because youth-oriented programs strengthened communities. "I see many people who appreciate what the YMCA has done for their lives," said Robbert. The core values of the YMCA serving North Simcoe are caring, honesty, inclusiveness, respect, and responsibility. Robbert strongly believed in a charity with values dedicated to providing opportunities for growth in spirit, mind, and body.

In 1963 Robbert became chairman of that year's Midland YMCA campaign. He wrote an advertisement for the campaign in the *Free Press Herald:*

> Once a year, the Midland YMCA calls on you for financial support ... support that is so necessary in order that the Y can carry on its vital work in this town. This year, we are asking for $15,000 ... a portion of the amount needed each year to operate the Y. Perhaps more important than money though, is your leadership. The Y provides various programs for citizens of all ages, but it needs leaders to guide these programs ...When a canvasser calls on you next week, please remember what the Y is doing, or can do for you and yours, and support it generously with your time, your talents and your prayers — signed Y'sly and Sincerely yours, Robbert Hartog, Campaign Chairman.

The Campaign kicked off with a dinner at the Y, which was then located at 467 Hugel Avenue West in Midland. When Robbert addressed the volunteers, he said they should be "dedicated, committed, and have a sense of humor," if the campaign was to succeed. "Each canvasser should be fully conversant on what the campaign is all about before setting out knocking on doors." "Unless we are committed ourselves, we strike a false note when we approach other people," he warned. "We must also show a willingness to make a few sacrifices ourselves to increase our own givings. This has a multiplying effect on others ... [And he concluded] It won't be a successful campaign, even if we reach our objective, if we don't enjoy what we are doing." With Robbert at the helm, the campaign objective of $15,000 was met. He was jubilant over the results. He congratulated the citizens who gave generously in support of the Y. The campaign came to a close in November 1963, but not before Robbert sent in a personal cheque which he, "decided to keep as a final surprise."

In 1964 Robbert was once again chairman of the year's Y campaign. Charles Walton, chairman of the board of directors of the Midland YMCA, announced Robbert's appointment in October 1964. In selecting Robbert for the second year in a row, Charles said, "The board had chosen a man who is deeply interested in the work of the YMCA, and who knows of its importance in the community." The objective of the campaign was to again raise $15,000. The campaign was launched on Monday, October 26, 1964. In accepting the chairmanship, Robbert said he "was willing to do anything in his power to help such an organization as the YMCA."

In the late 1960s the need for a year-round swimming pool in the community was discussed and a committee was struck under the general chairmanship of Robbert. Most of the committee members were also associated with the Midland Y's Men's Club, of which Robbert was also a member. Robbert was president of the club in 1969 (and a member until 1979), and he chaired another successful YMCA campaign that year. This campaign raised funds for a new swimming pool, which was constructed at Little Lake Park. It was during this campaign that Robbert first met Reinhart Weber, who would be his friend for years to come. Robbert was canvassing for the campaign and he was not shy about asking for donations. He approached Reinhart very frankly for a contribution. This was the beginning of a number of campaigns that the two friends worked together on.

Robbert became president of the Midland YMCA board of directors in the early 1970s. To celebrate Midland's centennial year in 1978, the YMCA launched a capital campaign to raise funds to build a new facility at Little Lake Park, adjacent to the ten-year-old swimming pool. Robbert again chaired this campaign. The proposal included a double gymnasium, indoor track, racquet courts, activity rooms and a health club. In a letter to Thompson Newspapers Ltd. in April 1978, Robbert made his case for the campaign: "I have had a very active involvement with the YMCA in Midland and currently am the chairman of the Top Level Gift Division in the largest and most exciting financial campaign in the Midland area. The Y (which has nearly 25 per cent of all Midland families as members, a real tribute to the leadership role the Y has earned in this town) intends to build a new building ... The project is a $1.1 million one and the total amount to be raised from the public is approximately $800,000 — of which a minimum of $400,000 must be secured before construction can start ... This project has been carefully conceived and is receiving a most heartening response from the Midland region. It is a project that has excited the community and is well supported by local donors and industry and by others outside the community who wish to support the local endeavours." When completed in April 1979, the building replaced the YMCA's 51-year-old Hugel Avenue facility.

In recognition of the donation Robbert provided for this campaign, John Leitch, president of the Midland YMCA, wrote him a letter explaining, "This gift sets the pattern for others to follow and will enable us to replace our worn-out building with new and improved facilities which will continue to serve as a force for good in our community for another half century. These future generations join us in extending our appreciation to you for your interest and support in helping us to strengthen and uphold the moral character of youth and to sustain and deepen family unity."

In May 1978 the Y had hosted a victory celebration to mark the end of the campaign. Robbert sent out an invitation to all members of the Top Level Gift Division and all members of the Campaign Committee, inviting them along with their spouses to join him for a victory drink aboard his boat, *D'eendracht*, moored at Sunnyside Marina. Upon completion of the campaign, Robbert wrote, "The Y complex that Midland will have must be by far the best that exists anywhere in a city the size of Midland (or twice for that matter)." He succeeded as usual.

When Robbert acquired a new business in Cambridge and relocated to the eastern end of Galt in the early 1980s, he immediately became involved with the YMCA there. Robbert's arrival came at a critical time for the Cambridge YMCA, which was faced with an aging facility at 25 Queen's Square and a large debt. His positions at the Cambridge Y included chair of the Fundraising Committee, vice-chair and board chair. Robbert was able to single-handedly get community leaders committed to the YMCA and to garner their full support to redevelop the organization and update the facility. He recruited senior community leaders to contribute their time, talent, and financial support to the association. Robbert was a firm believer

Reporter photo by Rainer Leipscher

CAMPAIGN MEMBERS, local politicians and the press were invited to the Cambridge Family YMCA yesterday morning to survey the new Queen's Square facilities. Here, (second from left) Gary Gray, YMCA executive director describes some of the features of the YMCA's new gymnasium, which houses courts for basketball' volleyball and badminton.

that the Y's ongoing success hinged on more than financial contributions, however, and he recruited talented individuals to serve alongside him.

In 1981 when the Cambridge YMCA New Building Fund Campaign was proposed, Robbert unveiled a rendering for the $800,000 modernization and expansion program to commence the following year. This involved removal of the original building, built in 1911, to be replaced with a modern up-to-date facility plus the addition of a double gym, three regulation handball/racquetball courts, a new activities control centre, meeting and activity rooms, change rooms, an adult health services facility, and a large weight training and exercise area. Robbert was the Campaign General and Top Level chairman. He hosted a meeting to elicit donations and spoke about the campaign, giving an impassioned presentation on the proposed building. "Because I feel so strongly for this project, my company and myself are putting $100,000 towards this project," he proclaimed. He then turned to a representative from Allan-Bradley and said, "What about Allan-Bradley?" That company matched Robbert's pledge and donated all the electrical systems for the building. Robbert donated all of the plumbing needs for the facility. He continued around the table and by the end the campaign goal was nearly met. The revitalized facility was built on schedule. Gary Gray, executive director of the Cambridge Y at the time, said that Cambridge could not have campaigned the way they did without

Robbert's leadership and wisdom. When Gary started with the Y, they had a weak reputation and a small membership. Robbert turned this around.

Gary and Robbert became good friends after working together at the Y. He recalled a story of a trip the two of them took on Robbert's boat. One summer weekend the two of them travelled towards Parry Sound. Robbert started barbecuing a roast for dinner that night. They anchored and prepared the rest of the meal. Robbert pulled out the roast and it was dark black and looked very burnt. Gary felt embarrassed for Robbert because the rest of the meal was done to perfection. Then Robbert drew up the carving knife and cut away the black coating. Inside was the most delicious roast Gary had ever tasted. Robbert knew exactly what he was doing, and Gary realized he should never have doubted him.

One evening Gary and Robbert met with a company that specialized in fundraising for capital campaigns. The first thing Robbert wanted to talk about was the company's fee and how the company was going to be paid. The representative was loud and overbearing. He said that he dealt in American dollars. Robbert replied, "We do all our business in Canadian dollars." The man replied, "No, I work in American dollars." Robbert again said, "Maybe you didn't hear me, we do our business in Canadian dollars." Again the representative replied "American." Robbert asked him if he went to England, did his company use American dollars? The man said, "No, we use pounds." They went back and forth and neither man would back down. Finally Robbert replied, "If you do not work in Canadian dollars, then we do not use your company." About a day later Robbert received a call from the company saying it would be happy to deal in Canadian dollars. Robbert refused and said the company had had its chance. He did not suffer fools gladly and did not have the patience for such discussions.

Robbert was involved in the highest echelons of the Cambridge YMCA. By 1983 he was president of the board of directors. Gary said that Robbert was very good with budgets, which benefited any campaign he worked on. He was not interested in people looking good because they came in under budget; he was more interested in people who came as close to the budget as possible. Three years later he took part in the burning of the Cambridge YMCA mortgage. After the revitalization of the Y building, the agency was left with a large debt, but the New Building Fund Campaign enabled the Y to repay its debt to the city. Directors, staff, volunteers and guests watched as the paper was lit. Robbert was honoured that night for his important role in "leaving the association debt free," said Dave Carson, the Cambridge YMCA president. "You can attribute the success of the

Cambridge YMCA today [2009] to a lot of the work that he did back in the early 1980s, no question about that." When Carson presented Robbert with the highest award, a life membership, Robbert was quick to ensure that all of the other individuals who played an important role in the resurgence of the YMCA in Cambridge be recognized.

Looking back on Robbert's career, Gary Gray acknowledged that Robbert was a great supporter of people who needed help, and who were willing to assist themselves. He did not make anyone feel inferior. He also supported the YMCA because "he was very youth oriented." Robbert's belief in helping others and his focus on youth may have initially drawn him to the YMCA, but he fully immersed himself in the issues. "I think that his leadership and his ability to get to the heart of the issue and lead the group was probably the most outstanding contribution," Dave Carson commented. "He was really an outstanding leader and could think through the problems. It was great. He was just a magnificent guy."

Robbert left Cambridge when he sold his company in 1984. He remained interested in the organization's progress, however, and kept in touch with a number of the people he worked with. Responding to a letter from John Hancock, CEO of the Cambridge Y, in July 2007, Robbert wrote, "It is with pleasure I (as past Chair) receive your Bulletin announcing the getting together of the Kitchener and Cambridge YMCA. This will be the beginning of a very strong Y, who can then get the best people, the best systems, etc. — and thereby provide the best service ... If in the future I can be of help to Cambridge/Kitchener (I am not proposing a name!!) let me know." Robbert also kept in touch with Gary Gray when the latter relocated to the Sudbury YMCA. He would call Gary when he was going to be up in the area on his boat and they would meet. Gary was involved with a campaign at the Sudbury Y and Robbert gave a donation because he believed in Gary's work. Gary was also involved with a YMCA camp in the area. A sink spout at the camp broke, so Gary called Robbert to ask where he could find an 18-inch spout, which was difficult to find in his area. A couple of days later, one arrived in the mail. Robbert was just that kind of man.

Robbert was also involved in the YMCA at national and international levels. According to Richard Bailey (CEO, YMCA World Urban Network and former CEO of YMCA Canada), YMCA Canada coordinates with YMCA representatives from across the country to continually address issues facing the organization. The YMCA is a local organization and each Y is different in the way they serve the needs of their community. Each YMCA reports to the national board but is not run at the national level.

Robbert was able to see how the Y met the needs of each community it served. YMCA Canada was created for local Y's to come together and relate to the federal government and other federal bodies as well as world bodies. Robbert was a member of the Cambridge Y when he was nominated to be on the YMCA Canada National Board, which consisted of 24 people. The board usually met four times a year. Robbert was nominated for YMCA Canada because he "was well respected for his work in the local Cambridge YMCA," said Richard Bailey. Robbert could look at the balance sheet of any YMCA in the country and tell you more about it than most people.

Robbert held a number of leadership positions within YMCA Canada. He was a member of the National Board from 1984 to 1986. From 1986 to 1992 he was an officer of the National Board (only five people held this position each year). He was also vice-chairman on the National Board from 1988 to 1991. From 1984 to 1985 he was chairman of the Audit Committee of which he remained a member from 1986 to 1988 and again in 1991. He was a member of the Investment Committee, the Executive Committee, the CEO Appraisal and Compensation Committee, the Nominating Committee (a YMCA Canada Committee), and the

Robbert in Lima, Peru visiting with local YMCA members.

Geneva Park Committee. He was treasurer of the YMCA Canada National Board from 1986 to 1988. In May 1992 Robbert became a provisional member (an advisor to the board) of the Audit Committee and the Investment Committee, after he had stepped down from the board. From June 13 to 17, 1984, he attended the National YMCA Conference in Halifax. The purpose of this conference was to establish a countrywide consultation process to generate information, understanding, and enthusiasm.

In 1986, Robbert travelled with Gary Gray and Colette Malo (manager, International Understanding, for the YMCA of Metropolitan Toronto at the time) to Lima, Peru. The three of them visited the Lima YMCA and met extensively with the staff, board, and committee personnel to set a three-year plan for the city's Y. Robbert arrived on a different flight than Gary and when his plane landed on the tarmac, it experienced a mechanical problem and could not advance to the terminal. Colette explained that Robbert, like the other passengers, looked out the window to see what was going on. Within minutes, armed soldiers boarded the plane and pulled down the window shades shouting that this part of the airport was a military zone and therefore not for civilian eyes. After some time, a higher-ranking soldier boarded the plane and asked the men to disembark. They were then asked to help push the aircraft as far as the terminal. Colette reminisced at how "Robbert laughed at this example of bureaucratic thinking that had not allowed passengers to peek out of their little windows and then had passengers physically inside the military zone pushing the plane forward."

Gary was counting on Robbert to be the interpreter, given his fluency in multiple languages. Although Robbert did not speak Spanish, after one week into the trip he was translating. "He picked up the language that fast," noted Gary. While in Lima, they had to get to a meeting and Robbert said, "Let me pick the taxi." So he chose a Volkswagen Bug, an old, beat-up car. Three passengers fit in and Robbert said, "This guy should be able to get us there in time, look at the condition of this cab." They had a wild ride, but they got to the meeting on time. Gary was amazed at Robbert's ability to adapt when travelling. He recalled Robbert ordering at a restaurant early in the trip. He was not able to read the menu in Spanish, so he ran his finger down the menu. Wherever it stopped, that is what he ordered!

Colette recalled Robbert's uncanny ability to predict how the staff and volunteers at the Lima YMCA would behave. "Before a discussion of their project's budget (community work and services in one of the shantytowns on the hills overlooking the city), Robbert placed a bet with me: 'They will propose a much higher financial request than you had discussed with them.' 'Nonsense,' I said. Robbert was right. At the end of our stay of a few days, I had lost every single bet with him about the project. I don't know what to call that skill: experience, probably." When Robbert was talking to the staff about their budget, he asked why it was based on 19 people. The staff began defending the importance of the project. Robbert replied, "No, no. You misunderstand. I am asking why 19 people and not, let's say, 23." The mood in the room changed from defensiveness to an open-minded questioning of the personnel needs.

During the discussions, Colette was doing simultaneous translation and therefore had limited opportunities to contribute her own views. "Whenever the Peruvians said something that Robbert particularly approved of, he would thrust both hands out and make a [plus symbol] with his two

Left: The taxi in Peru Robbert handpicked to get him and his fellow travelers to a meeting on time. Robbert (far right) during his trip to Peru with the YMCA.

index fingers," she recalled. "Every time he did this, his audience flinched. I finally had to stop all discussion and ask what it meant to them when Robbert made his plus. To him the gesture represented a 'plus' sign and meant 'well done.' To them it represented a 'cross' and signified death." That was one occasion when he didn't read the room correctly.

Robbert travelled extensively for business and for various volunteer projects. He was well acquainted with the international scene — he knew background information about various countries and their cultures and was able to interpret this information. "His capability for thinking, sorting through complex issues, and making them simple, bringing diversity of thought to the issues that were being discussed made him a person whom people valued," said Richard Bailey. The depth and breadth of Robbert's knowledge of global economics, politics, and social issues enriched his involvement with the Y at both national and international levels.

In the late 1980s, shortly after joining the YMCA Canada National Board of Directors, Robbert was selected to represent Canada on the World Alliance of YMCAs. The World Alliance fosters strategic partnerships with a range of international agencies, including other youth organizations, United Nations agencies and ecumenical partners. It was prestigious to be selected to represent Canada on the World Alliance.

From 1988 to 1992 Robbert was on the World Alliance Finance Committee. He was also a representative on the Executive Committee and chairperson of the World Alliance Advisory Committee. Robbert attended conferences in Aruba, Korea, and Switzerland. The gatherings were held a week at a time. World Councils hosted 500 to 600 people from around the globe. Don McCreesh, former chair of the board of YMCA Canada, worked with Robbert at the national and international levels and attended several World Alliance meetings with Robbert. As the Canadian representatives, they referred to themselves as "heretics" since the YMCA is very much a Christian, evangelical organization in other areas of the world. In Canada the YMCA adopted a more secular position. Accordingly, the Canadian YMCA had problems with the World Alliance. Don recalled that it was becoming political, involving liberation theology. There was also a youth movement in the organization and to have a retired senior citizen with a heavy Dutch accent representing Canada took some members aback. Don and Robbert explained to other committee members that they were both immigrants, which is reflective of Canada. Soon Robbert bonded with the youth on the council. He did not go out of his way to do this; he simply included them in conversations. Don explained:

> Robbert didn't have a dynamic sort of charismatic leadership style to get accepted. He would just appear on the scene, start asking some very detailed questions, and suddenly people would start to acknowledge, 'Hey, this guy knows what he's talking about'... He would be very soon recognized for thoughtful leadership in terms of knowledge and where it could go, and also integrity. It took him a lot less time to get accepted at the World Executive for those reasons. He would take that pragmatic business approach to things. It didn't take people long to realize he wasn't political, he didn't want to play games, he just wanted to do the right thing.

Robbert approached his role on the World Alliance as a global citizen bringing his experience with Canadian Executive Service Organization (CESO) into his work on the World Alliance, especially on issues in South East Asia. During one meeting, Robbert could tell that some Central American countries were playing up their plight. Robbert answered them in Spanish to challenge them on it. "He understood what was going on in those kind of communities," said Don. When they travelled, Don noted that Robbert would dress down and would try to fit in with the people with whom they were working. "If you ever met Robbert on the street, you would never know he was as successful as he was," Don reflected. "He didn't have that whole presence kind of thing, that was never a big deal with him. He just wanted to go out, contribute, and have fun. To feel at the end of the day he had made the world a better place."

Robbert never saw himself as a leader at YMCA Canada. He simply thought about what was right for the organization. He would know if he was the right person for the chairman position. "He got positions not for being political, but for being effective," said Don. Robbert always focused on the social mission of the YMCA, and this made him an important volunteer at all levels of the organization.

Robbert returned to Midland in 1984 and he again became involved with the local Y. In June 1994 he was recognized as a volunteer for his 31st year of service to the Midland YMCA. Five years later the Midland Y's Men's Club made Robbert an Honorary Life Member. "It was extremely kind of the Midland YMCA to give me an Honorary Life Membership Award," Robbert said. "The Y has played an important role in our community, thanks to the dedication of many people." He highly prized this honour, and even more the friendship with so many.

According to Jim Commerford (president and CEO, YMCA of Barrie, Midland, Collingwood and Orillia and YMCA of Cobourg at the time), Robbert had the ability to look ahead and see where they were going and he believed in the consolidation of the Y boards. The Midland YMCA was one of four in the region. In 1998 Midland joined the Barrie/Orillia YMCA group, followed by Collingwood, which joined in 2001. That year there were negotiations to create a new common board of directors, still with four separate corporations. In 2007, the Simcoe/Muskoka amalgamated board was created. Robbert helped to bridge the gap to allow people in Midland to feel that their concerns were met. "Robbert had an innate ability to look back at history, allow it to influence and learn from it in terms of what needs to be done in today's context," Jim explained. "But the other unique aspect that made him the type of man he was, was he put it really in the framework of looking to the future." Robbert's influence was not in the forefront, but through quiet persuasion and listening. "That was Robbert Hartog," said Jim. "He was the rainmaker of the YMCA."

Robbert supported the Sponsorship Fund set up by the Midland YMCA to enable people with more modest income to participate fully in the activities for the Y, while enabling the institution to provide quality services. He was an enthusiastic contributor to the fund and he approached like-minded people to solicit their contribution. In 2000, he was the co-chair for the Sponsorship Fund. That year Robbert wrote,

> The Sponsorship Fund is a very important aspect of the YMCA and it makes its facility and programs accessible to everyone in our North Simcoe community, including families that are less fortunate than ourselves. This remains a core value of the YMCA movement ...

Today, 463 individuals are being supported by the Fund, over half are youth. It is through this fund that a child can participate in a summer day camp, learn to swim, play sports after school or an adult can gain a healthier lifestyle. Of those assisted, most are also contributing towards their program, in the most unfortunate situations, the Fund is pleased to contribute the full amount. In all cases, the YMCA carefully assesses the individual's ability to contribute.

Robbert continued to donate to the fund for several years.

John McCullough (chair of the board of governors of Georgian College) volunteered with Robbert at the Midland YMCA. He acknowledged that people often focus on Robbert's financial contribution, but he also contributed through his determination to see things succeed and encouraged other people to become involved. He said Robbert's draw to organizations such as the Y was "his interest in people and bettering people"— he believed in the growth of the mind, body and spirit through the YMCA. All the while, "he wanted absolutely no recognition, that was Robbert: 'I'm not doing it for me, I'm doing it for the community.'" In 2001, however, the YMCA recognized Robbert as a "companion" in the YMCA Canada Fellowship of Honour — the highest honour that can be bestowed on an individual within the YMCA. In response to this recognition, Robbert wrote, "As so many people, I have received much more from the Y than what I have invested in it. While I have serious doubts about my qualifications for this fellowship, it is nevertheless an honour from an organization I admired, and therefore is an honour I cherish."

On November 19, 2001, Robbert, with his guest Guusje Parks, attended a second vice-regal reception at Rideau Hall in Ottawa where Her Excellency, the Right Honourable Adrienne Clarkson, Governor General

Robbert receiving the YMCA Canada Fellowship of Honour from Governor General Adrienne Clarkson. (2001)

Robbert (front row, far right) with other YMCA honourees at Rideau Hall in 2001.

of Canada, awarded him the Fellowship after more than four decades of volunteering. "It was a nice day and the Governor General is a very charming person," said Robbert. "It was an honour to be there." The program for the event praised Robbert for his support of the YMCA:

> Robbert greatly impacted our people, programs, operations and structure. He has introduced sound business principles, clearly demonstrating that fiscal responsibility and humanitarianism are equally critical to our sustained growth and viability… He has mentored, encouraged, inspired and challenged countless individuals into a life of service with the YMCA and the broader community. With one eye always focused on the future, Robbert strives to instill YMCA values in those he deems to be our next generation of leaders. Many have drawn energy and inspiration from him, and consider themselves privileged to have worked side by side with a man of such high repute.

Robbert continued to quietly support the Midland Y. Tom Coon (CEO of YMCA Simcoe/Muskoka) said Robbert always made time for him. He was continually astounded by Robbert's network of contacts. "I chalk it up to Robbert's values and his incredible interest in people's welfare," said Tom. "He always had his antennae up and would hear about stuff, and if it was important he would do something about it, or make sure you did something."

In May 2003, Robbert felt it was time to take action to help the local Y once again. He and Reinhart Weber (who was the force behind the Youth Leadership Program) made an anonymous offer to fund the entire cost of a proper professional engineering/architectural study of the Midland Y building to determine what should be done to upgrade and improve the facilities. The Midland Y had a 35-year-old building, which was built within a strict budget, and therefore the facility would need repairs and enhancements.

Robbert and Reinhart collaborated with Ralph Befort (fellow Midland industrialist and a former Scout of Robbert's) for a campaign to assist with Y upgrades. In 2005 the Strong Kids, Strong Families, Strong Communities Campaign was launched in support of the Midland YMCA. Robbert was patron of the campaign. The campaign needed $4 million to complete needed improvements to the facility, including a new, larger, licensed child care space, as well as a non-licensed child-minding program space, new and larger program spaces to allow the facility to serve more individuals in program areas where space is limited, new fitness and individual conditioning space to provide more opportunities for individuals to participate in a bright, open space, with more equipment, a group biking studio, and individual counselling areas, new locker rooms with a clean and updated look to provide more privacy and to serve those with special needs, and a new social space to provide a comfortable area for parents to meet children and friends after their workout.

In a letter dated January 23, 2006, Tom Coon and Robert Reid (chair of the board of directors, YMCA Simcoe/Muskoka) announced,

The YMCA of Midland located at 560 Little Lake Park Road.

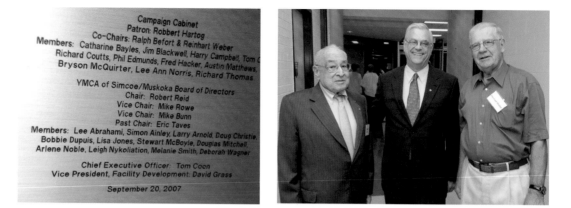

Right inset (left to right): Robbert, Tom Coon, and Reinhart Weber at a YMCA function.

Top left and bottom right: The donor wall at the YMCA of Midland with Robbert's name listed as a Patron.

with a great sense of accomplishment and appreciation, that the campaign had realized its ambitious $4 million fundraising goal. Tom noted that Robbert's involvement with the campaign never waned. Thanks to the efforts of Robbert, Reinhart, and Ralph Befort (Reinhart and Ralph were campaign co-chairs), the capital campaign reached its target. Ralph explained,

> Nobody ever thought that this area could handle a $4.2 million capital campaign. People that did this for a living said there's no way the demographics of this community could handle that. Not only did we do a $4.2 million campaign, but right afterwards my wife [Kathy Befort], she is the president of the Hospital Foundation, handled a $6.2 million dollar campaign and it was extremely successful and finished as well, thanks to Robbert and Reinhart again on that one … When people said it can't be done, the two of them really proved on an ongoing basis that anything can be done when you put your mind to it. And it is not like they just wrote cheques, they did, but

their pizzazz and enthusiasm were contagious. And people say the three of us were like that, and I don't know what I looked like or did to add to that chemistry, but I was proud to be part of it.

Ralph had a great deal of respect for Robbert since his youth as a member of Robbert's Scout troop. Of his experience on the campaign he said, "Robbert was a very good mentor through that process. You never know you need mentoring … When you go through a process like that you are a better person afterwards for spending time with an individual with such a great amount of knowledge, experience, know-how, wisdom, and you just feel bigger, stronger, smarter when you are done."

The Midland Y renovations were scheduled to be complete by 2006. In 2007, Robbert wrote to Tom, "It was most pleasing to note that the new Y will be a first-class building — excellent quality all around, and all I could have hoped for." Robbert was particularly proud of the community's efforts. "It's a good feeling to know that even though I can't use all of the new facilities, other people can. And isn't that the point of giving?"

Robbert continually tried to better his community and he valued what the YMCA contributed to the lives of local citizens. He also understood the importance of national and international Y governing bodies to organize at a larger level. Through his involvement and financial contributions, Robbert provided direction, stability, and inspiration to his local YMCAs and to all levels of the organization.

Top: Robbert in a casual discussion with a YMCA staff member after an annual meeting.

Below: Robbert (third from the left) and Reinhart (fourth from the left) in the crowd at the YMCA Annual General Meeting in 2007.

CHAPTER FIVE

A Spirit of Adventure

Starting at Sioux Lookout, Robbert Hartog travelled under a railway trestle, headed northeast across Pelican Lake to Pelican Falls (a rapid that can be easily run, especially for an experienced canoeist), and into the English River. From there he crossed the eastern end of Lac Seul and used his compass to point southeast of Tukegweik Bay. It became difficult to identify the shoreline. Miles later, after ascending Root River to Nottaway Falls, hard paddling was needed to combat the two-mile-per-hour current. This river led to the first portage, and the remains of an old marine railway and cabin.

On an August day in 1978, about 30 days after starting out at Sioux Lookout, 650 miles and over 30 portages later, Robbert's paddle touched the fast-flowing waters of the Albany River. Along with six other skillful canoeists, Robbert ventured to the old trading post waters of the Hudson's Bay Company, with a history dating back to 1683. At 59 years of age he had covered a route that called for the utmost caution, with its many rapids, swift water, and demanding portages. At this time of his life, canoeing was addictive for Robbert. The vast wildlife, the thrill of exploration, the companionship of fellow adventurers, and the breathtaking views of Canada's wilderness provided a fulfilling summer vacation for the Waltec company president. With the first snowfall of winter each year, Robbert began planning for the next summer's trip.

Canoeing through the remote Canadian wilderness.

According to his personal records, Robbert canoed the Spanish River in the 1960s; he went on a "giant canoe trip from the Moose River crossing to Penetanguishene, in 1969" with the Midland Rovers; in 1972 he canoed the Albany River; in 1974 he travelled to the South Nahanni; in 1980 from Webequie to Winisk; in 1981 from Big Trout Lake to Fort Severn, along Fawn River; in 1982 from Pickle Lake to the Attawapiskat; and in 1983 along the Moisie River at the Quebec-Labrador border. He travelled along many other rivers in his time: the Attawapiskat was "really the only major Ontario river ending in James/Hudson Bay that I have not yet run," he said before embarking on his trip there. The trips often required 32 to 35 kilometres of paddling a day. He was in good physical condition for the demanding trips. As the years passed Robbert would often throw his back out while canoeing, but he never complained.

Robbert's big trip to the South Nahanni River in the Northwest Territories took place in August 1974. With seven friends (John Bell, Ed Brook, Bart Brophy, Waxy Gregoire, Evan Monkman, Bill Moore, and Eric Mundinger), Robbert travelled from the Moose Ponds to Nahanni Butte. The men

Above: Robbert dipping his paddle into one of Canada's beautiful lakes.

Right: The intimidating and breathtaking scenery of the Nahanni.

on the trip ranged in age from 23 to 63. The South Nahanni is one of the most beautiful rivers in Canada, but it has challenging waters that are rarely travelled. There is a myth that the waters are cursed. According to a study by Parks Canada, the wild, uninhabited country is responsible for a number of "mysterious deaths." The study showed that between 1904 and 1973, at least 20 people drowned, starved, froze or simply disappeared.

On the trips, Robbert often took people from Midland who had never been in a canoe before. There was a core group involved that was older, but John Bell recalled that "he took on some very tough kids from Midland," such as Lawrence (Waxy) Gregoire (23 years old at the

The canoeists stopping for a break.

time), who had very long hair and was different than the rest of the group. Waxy and Patrick (Bart) Brophy compiled a logbook of the trip. In the foreword they say,

> One cannot achieve full satisfaction simply by reading of this well-known river. He must be there to breathe the cool, crisp morning air; he must be there to smell the scent of vast stands of spruce and poplar and the odours of yet another well-cooked meal. He must be right there on the Nahanni to feel the strain of portaging lining and hard paddling to beat its numerous eddies and swift current. And most important of all, much more desirable than the aforementioned, is that one must be there to feel the tenseness, the excitement and challenge of its unexpected, fast-approaching white waters … The wild is calling.

On Thursday, August 8, 1974, Waxy and Bart's log reads,

> Again Boss [Robbert] was cooking breakfast in the rain. What would we have done without him? But before the last canoeist rose, the sky had cleared so breakfast was served at 7:30 a.m. under the sun. Orange juice, mushroom omelet, oatmeal with fruit and almonds and coffee prepared our stomachs for the morning ahead. By the time the

morning chores were completed, it was 9:15 a.m. The river had slowed down somewhat but we paddled another 20 miles through very winding, tumbling waters. Travelling close to the mountains is breathtaking and we were moving at such a speed that we could enjoy every different angle of the same rock formation; and believe us, there are some awe-inspiring formations to be encountered. Today we've had the best day weatherwise since the start of the trip. We stopped a few times on the river for short rests and energy candies, but kept paddling until we reached our predetermined campsite.

The next day the canoeists travelled close to the falls. Waxy and Bart wrote,

Most of us have been on several trips before and some were pretty rough but never were we so quiet as this morning heading towards Virginia Falls. It seemed odd that all four canoes were a mere three or four feet from the banks of the river. We were clinging to it as though it were our only friend in the world. We were playing it very cautious. We passed CWS camp and could see the old barge on the shore which marked the beginning of the portage. It is not until you are around the last bend that one is able to hear the roar of the falls. Once that bend is passed you can see a heavy mist hanging just above the falls and the closer you get to them, the louder the thunder of the falling water becomes. The portage is just 150 feet away from the rapids at the crest of the cataract and we clung to the shore until we reached the barge. No way did we want to drift a single foot past that landing — just no way! That would mean a 300-foot fall into a wet grave.

Robbert travelled these rivers at the age of 55. John Bell recalled the high degree of difficulty and challenging waters with waterfalls "twice as high as Niagara." At that time, few people had travelled the Nahanni, which is now a provincial Park. John recalled,

One of the most traumatic things that happened to us, he [Robbert] was in the stern and I was in the bow and we went through canyons that were miles long and the water was very frigid. They traversed the river to the left side, keeping together in case one canoe was in danger.

Top: Robbert (also known as "Boss") preparing breakfast.

Below: The canoeists gather before heading out for the day.

Robbert (right) navigating
through rough waters.

John and Robbert were in the last canoe. Waxy and Bart recalled, "A wave hit them broadside as they were making the cut and they were almost able to recover. Unfortunately, a second wave hit and swamped the canoe. They bailed out but clung to the canoe. The water was frigid and moving very fast. Boss lost his grip and started to swim for shore while John managed to stay with the canoe as it floated through the rapids. We had to get them to shore before they were channelled into the Third Canyon, for there was nowhere to land within five miles beyond this part." John said, "I drifted down the river for what seemed like miles … and I remember them taking me out and it was frigid cold and they said, 'Where's Robbert?' I remember very clearly I was sure he was dead because the last I saw his head was going under. So I said 'Oh well, he's back up there,' because I didn't want to shock them, I didn't want to be the guy that delivered the bad news that Robbert was dead."

According to Waxy and Bart,

They then "headed towards Boss and pulled him closer to shore, where Eric threw him a rope. Eric and Evan pulled him to safety while Waxy and Bart paddled further to rescue a food pack which had broken loose. Ed and Bill, in the meantime, were mustering their muscular brawn to inch their way to shore, dragging John and a water-filled canoe behind them … Boss and John stood shivering and dripping, but all in one piece. We had lost two paddles but this is where spares come in handy. It was quite an ordeal for those two. An episode not to be forgotten for years to come." John remembers the men started a fire and he and Robbert shivered away. "This was the days before waterproof things, so we were wet as can be … That was a life-changing event." After this trip, John remembered Robbert developing a cough that he had for many years.

Many of the areas Robbert travelled to, including the Nahanni, were remote and transportation into the areas was primarily by air. Robbert would organize the airline tickets, the often elaborate arrangements for the transportation of the canoes, and the rendezvous points for various passengers from Midland, Cambridge, Huntsville, and other cities and towns. Before the trips, Robbert would often contact local tourism offices to prepare his group for the many unknowns that they could encounter on the water. In preparation for the Moisie River trip, he corresponded with Quebec Tourism with letters written in French. The Ministry of Natural Resources also provided support for the trips with its Canoe Trip Reports. After travelling to the Attawapiskat, Robbert wrote the ministry with suggestions to improve the reports by keeping the information up to date and accurate. He felt that an already useful service could become even more helpful with additional information.

For each of his trips three to seven fellow canoeists and friends accompanied Robbert. He always handled all of the logistics for the trips. "Robbert was always the boss on those trips," said Bill Moore, who travelled to the

A seaplane (sometimes the only way to access the remote areas Robbert traveled) drops off the canoeists to begin their journey.

Nahanni with Robbert. In his letters planning the trips, he would always leave an open invitation for "other good campers and pleasant persons" who would like to join them. Robbert researched and planned the trips down to their smallest detail, from ordering freeze-dry shrimp creole, beef stew, and chocolate cream pudding to organizing the tent groups. For the eight-man trip to Winisk he was sure to specify that a two-man Gore-Tex tent would be available "for the heavy snorers!" He was also meticulous in assuring that proper first aid gear was available. For the same trip he specified that he would need some Adrenalin packed for his bee sting allergy. In order to keep supplies and luggage loads to a minimum for the portages, Robbert sent out a list of possible personal equipment in the weeks leading up to departure. His load always worked out to within about a half-pound of the suggested weight — if not right on! For a 3 ½ week trip, for example, he specified: 3 nylon shorts, 2 nylon "topper" shirts, 1 long-sleeved woollen sweater, 1 rain pants, 2 pairs of socks, 4 hankies, and several more minimal items. When it came to control of the weather for the trips, Robbert tried to delegate that job, as he said, "We will need someone to arrange for a warm spell during the canoeing period — whoever we can trust in that regard!!"

Although fishing was not his primary focus, he was optimistic for the other travellers who hoped to make a contribution to dinner. Before the Albany trip, Robbert joked that there would be "opportunity for a bit of fishing … I won't say catching fish." On the Fawn River trip the water was reportedly "either too murky, too clear, too cold or too warm, too fast or too slow," but that didn't stop the fishermen from providing some excellent meals. On that trip, pickerel and northern pike were plentiful, but trout were much harder to come by.

In many of the northern areas explored by Robbert and his friends, there were only signs of occasional use of the river by humans. Visible landmarks such as a trapper's cabin, a hunting camp, or small graveyards were scarce. What the areas lacked in human contact, however, they surely made up for in animal species. On the Winisk trip a polar bear posed for a picture. Along Fawn River the canoeists spotted beaver, muskrat, otter, mink, bear, and moose. The group gave the name Sylvester to a seal that provided two hours of amusement as it played about in the water while the men set up camp. Geese, ducks, trumpeter swans, loons and

An early morning fog rolls in during breakfast.

Robbert's canoe trips were well-organized, challenging, and full of adventure.

curlews dotted the water as the canoes glided through the rivers. On one trip, Robbert realized he forgot his camera after a very long portage. He walked back along the path to retrieve it and he looked over a ledge and saw a very rare bison.

Robbert's experiences on the mighty rivers of northern Canada allowed him to expand his appreciation for nature. This passion for Canadian wilderness continued throughout his life.

Although the last canoe trip he recorded was in 1983, he continued to enjoy life on the water with his upsized travelling companion: the yacht *D'eendracht*. In the late 1940s T.G. (Tom) Drew-Brook suggested to Robbert that he take up boating on Georgian Bay, to relax from the pressures of business. Robbert followed this advice. After that time, he crossed the bay, by powerboat, by canoe, while camping ashore or living aboard — and enjoyed it all. Over the years Robbert owned three boats: *Sea Flight, Clytie*, and *D'eendracht*. The latter was named after the boat which Robbert's ancestor Dirk Hartog sailed in 1616 when he was the first white person to set foot on Australia. (On a trip to Australia, Robbert was flown to Cape Inscription on Dirk Hartog Island to visit the pewter plate nailed to a post that Dirk left behind to record his visit to western Australia.) When Robbert moved to Midland in 1962, he was able to spend more time on his boat. In the summer of 1979, during one of his best boating seasons, he spent three weeks and nearly every weekend on his boat.

Above and Below: *Clytie* traveling on Georgian Bay.

Robbert also loved to explore. As captain of his boat he travelled throughout the Great Lakes and he circumnavigated Newfoundland and also toured the Greek Islands. But he spent most of his time on the waters close to home on Georgian Bay, the large bay of Lake Huron, consisting of tens of thousands of islands. The beautiful scenery on the water inspired many paintings done by Canadian artists, the Group of Seven. Robbert saw Georgian Bay as his own backyard — he knew every corner of it and was always willing to give advice on safe anchorages and to swap stories with fellow boaters. The Canadian Coast Guard recognized Robbert's skill and appointed him a Volunteer Search Master, thus allowing him to fly their pennant. The Great Lakes Cruising Club also recognized Robbert's knowledge of the lakes and awarded him their Admiral Bay Award.

A captain with such an immense understanding of his surroundings was a joy for any crew. Each summer Robbert would assemble a crew for various weekends or long trips by sending out a letter to a number of his friends and family. One of Robbert's greatest pleasures was entertaining aboard his boat. In his invitation letter Robbert would list several weekends and destinations, and the corresponding dates. Many of the trips were around Georgian Bay, but often he planned a longer trip; for example, in 1997 he travelled up Lake Superior to Thunder Bay. He would include a form to be returned to him on which he would have his friends and family list their top three date choices, their preferred time of departure and return, and other remarks.

Robbert had cross-generational appeal. He enjoyed seeing the various people from all aspects of his life mingling on his boat. Often his family members would accompany him on board. Robbert was the proud uncle of ten nieces and nephews and a great uncle to over twenty great nieces and nephews. His nephew Ronald Schokking said, "It was always amazing that on the one hand Robbert was a strict business man and well organized, while on the other hand he could relax with his own family. He particularly enjoyed seeing the kids." His niece Beatrice Brom remembers going on Robbert's boat as a child: "His boat trips … were the greatest fun, and with his big smiles to us as children, an uncle who related to us differently than a demanding parent, and his contagious laugh." Robbert's family lived in countries all over the world, but he cherished family gatherings, special

Robbert docking *Clytie*.

The picturesque Georgian Bay.

A temporary crew after a day's outing on the water with Robbert.

occasions, and any opportunity to get together. His niece Yvonne Mansell recalls how Robbert "knew his nieces and nephews very well, and would remember what each of our strengths were. He would also tease us. During his visits he would connect with each of us, asking questions about our music or sports, our school and friends, and even though he didn't spend a long time, because of how he related to us, the connection was real." Robbert stayed close with his family throughout his life and he enjoyed the opportunity to travel with them and entertain them aboard his boat.

His vast network of friends meant that at any given time he would have a unique mixture of people of different backgrounds. This made for interesting conversation on everything from philosophy to the weather. Robbert would match up couples and singles at random (depending on their weekend availability), unless cruising partners were specifically requested. This system allowed Robbert's friends to mingle and get to know one another. He sent a "Preliminary Cruising Confirmation" letter in the spring, welcoming his friends aboard his boat for a specified duration and destination. The letters benefited from advancing technology: plain, typewritten text in the late 1970s was upgraded to include colours, tables, and even clip art in the late 1990s!

Depending on the crew aboard, a typical evening on the boat featured Robbert cooking a delicious meal, followed by several bridge games. Although there were many crew hands to pitch in and help, he was very insistent that there was only to be one cook. Several women who tried to help out quickly learned that they were not welcome in Robbert's kitchen. He would, however, let someone else play bartender. Robbert was particular about where everything was, especially aboard his boat. If someone started moving things around, he would be displeased. This became more obvious as he got older. When some of Robbert's former Scouts travelled with him on his summer trips they would bring their wives along. The women were not always accustomed to Robbert's way of doing things, so they would often hear a growl or comment when something was moved or done differently. Meanwhile, the Scouts had known Robbert's way of conduct on the boat since their youth.

D'eendracht was made up of three staterooms, (two double, one single), two heads with a shower/toilet, and a convertible double sofa in the salon. It was a beautiful 53-foot-11-inch Cliff Richardson boat. Guusje Parks described the ending of an August 1998 trip as *D'eendracht* made its way to Britt: "Always an interesting trip — past so many streaks of islands. The docking went perfect — Bravo Robbert! What a wonderful time we all have had. Tremendous crew — many laughs, excellent meals, beautiful weather, gorgeous scenery. What more could you want!" Many friends echoed these sentiments, years later, as they recalled their fond memories.

On June 20, 1999, around 1:00 p.m., while travelling to Britt down a channel, Robbert had an accident that badly damaged *D'eendracht's* hull. According to Robbert he "hit, what must have been a sharp pinnacle —

Top: Captain Robbert steering *D'eendracht*.
Bottom: *D'eendracht* anchored in Georgian Bay.

which by chance, sliced a tear along the weld line, just below the engine compartment. This resulted in heavy water spray into the engine air intake and thus into the caterpillars." Ruth Rowland (a long-time friend of Robbert's who was aboard the boat at the time) said one of the markers on the shoal had blown off or moved and the boat hit the rock "with a terrible bang." The water level in the lakes that year had dropped and Robbert was aware of this. He always had full control of his environment and he was particularly shaken by the accident. The boat began to take on water as the pumps gave out. Robbert needed help to get his boat to Doug Wright's nearby dock. He received "some spontaneous and willing and most efficient help from a group of volunteers," for which he was very appreciative. An outboard aluminum boat came to tow the boat to the marina. The repairs took longer than he hoped, and he had to cancel the boat trips scheduled for the rest of that summer. Robbert wrote a letter explaining the situation to his boating friends, which he concluded

Robbert with friends aboard
his boat.

saying, "I do hope the necessity of cancelling trips in 1999 will not discourage you to come along in 2000!" He said, "It was a freak accident, with freak results — (I cannot calculate the probabilities of all this happening so precisely) and I can only hope for a lucky 2000!"

Robbert planned a trip from Britt to Thunder Bay in the summer of 2000, but unfortunately, this would mark the last year he captained a boat. At the beginning of September he found several minor yet important problems with *D'eendracht*, which he found difficult to contend with. Therefore, he reluctantly decided to discontinue the season. In a conversation with his nephew Ronald Schokking, Robbert simply said, "Well that's it." His adventures on the boat had been great, but it was time to move on. This reflected his general outlook on life. When he sold Waltec Enterprises Ltd. he did not get too emotional; rather, he made a rational decision and moved on. Ronald said this was "typical of Robbert: when it's done, it's done and you move on." At the time, Robbert simply said, "It is the best thing to do." In a letter to his friends, dated September 20, 2000, Robbert explained his decision:

> For 26 years now *D'eendracht* was my floating cottage and the Great Lakes (and the Seaway) became home waters. Thanks to my many friends, who joined in the crossing work and pleasure, the joy of boating multiplied. Thank you all very much for your presence and friendship. The time has come now to end this boating life, as I do not feel I can guarantee safe passage and timely return to harbour under all circumstances. I will miss it, but will especially miss your presence aboard. However, other activities will no doubt replace the traditional ones. You will not receive a spring invitation to select a date. *D'eendracht* is now for sale but my memories of the many friends on *D'eendracht* will continue. Thank you for all the joys you added to the various voyages.

Many of his friends replied with words of thanks. Bette and Tom Gibson wrote to Robbert, saying, "It has been five decades of indescribable memories. Sharing the warm sun, the winds, the majestic scenery, friendship and frolic with you and your intrepid crew. This has been very much a wonderful slice of our lives and one so few have the opportunity to be a part of." In the following years Robbert would reflect back on his summers on the boat, and he would often mention his fond memories of these times in letters to friends around Christmas time. He realized that the summers on the water were a unique chance to get together with friends on a regular basis. He truly missed this.

D'eendracht was for sale for a number of years. In the fall of 2002 Chapman School of Seamanship (a recognized U.S. charity) was willing (anxious even) to take it over for an agreed value with a charitable receipt. Jennifer Castle Field, president of Chapman School of Seamanship (a private, non-profit educational institution), thanked Robbert and explained that these gifts were vital to the school "in continuing to provide quality education in the marine industry." Furthermore, she expressed that the goal of the school "has been to meet the changing and expanding educational and training needs of professional mariners as well as recreational boating youth and adults." The transfer was completed in 2003.

A pensive Robbert looks out on the lake he referred to as his own backyard.

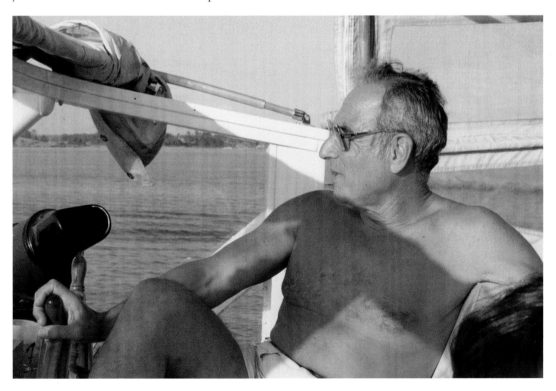

CHAPTER SIX

Skip Hartog and Scouting

In the early 1960s Robbert Hartog was the Scoutmaster of the 81st Toronto Sea Scout Group. This troop met in the basement of Rosedale United Church in Toronto. In the summer, many Scouts had the privilege of attending Robbert's summer camp north of Manitoulin Island. The boys would board Robbert's yacht in Penetanguishene, bristling with excitement as they headed out into the "wild seas of Georgian Bay." They headed north to Little Current for supplies, and then crossed the straits to the beaches of their encampment on the mainland. They camped overnight en route and rose early each morning with an inspection of the site by Robbert, known to the Scouts as "Skipper" or "Skip" Hartog.

Each Scout had the discipline of doing his own part with the team as they packed up. They arrived at their destination onshore to discover no campground at all, soon realizing that this would not be a summer resort camp. They were led to clear the campsite and unfurl ghastly canvas army surplus tents. The Scouts worked to stay dry and fed. They cooked their meals on the campfire and took regular hikes into the hills. A reward for hiking to the "mountains" in intense heat was the chilling thrill of diving into mineral turquoise lakes at the trails' end. There was much to do each

An aerial view of the 1977 Scout Jamboree in Prince Edward Island.

A make-shift boy scout camp.

day, which kept the boys busy. They learned various knots and enthusiastically lashed and tied rope beds and chairs. To provide for the fires and clear the sites they endlessly chopped wood. There was downtime when each of the boys took turns water-skiing off Robbert's tender or supply tender. They lined up for the chance to learn how to operate those same craft on ship-to-shore missions. Many boys wished this experience went on forever.

Robbert's history with Scouting dates back to 1932, when he became a Scout in Versailles, France, at the age of 13. In 1938 he became Assistant Scoutmaster of the 3rd Versailles and then Scoutmaster of the 1st Versailles until 1940. That year he was involved with the France National Headquarters for Scouting as the acting general secretary of the Eclaireurs Unionistes de France. After Robbert had moved to Canada to study at the University of Toronto, he reconnected with Scouting and became Scoutmaster for the 113th Toronto Glenmoore from October 1940 to July 1943. When he went to Europe in 1943 he became Delegate of Royal Commissioner and Acting Commissioner from September 1943 to January 1945. After the war, he once again became Scoutmaster of the 113th Glenmoore and then a Rover Scout leader the following year. For the next four decades Robbert remained thoroughly involved in Scouting in the communities in which he lived, and at the national and international levels.

Scouts Canada is a not-for-profit organization, and the country's leading youth organization for boys and girls age 5 to 26. Scouting is the world's largest voluntary youth movement, as countries with individual programs form part of the collective World Organization of the Scout Movement. All over the world, youths are provided with opportunities to find a meaningful place in society and to practice leadership in a positive setting. The values of Scouts are expressed by the Scouting promise and law, familiar to any Scout: "On my honour I promise that I will do my best; To do my duty to God and the Queen; To help other people at all times, And to carry out the spirit of the Scout Law. A Scout is helpful and trustworthy, kind and cheerful, considerate and clean, wise in the use of all resources."

Robbert was a strong volunteer for Scouts Canada, and over the years took on a number of responsibilities. For example, he was a member of the Toronto District Executive and Greater Toronto Region Executive from 1948 to 1962. In 1952 he was acting district commissioner of the

St. George's District, and he held various volunteer positions in this area throughout the 1950s to early 1960s. He was Sea Scout master of the 81st Toronto Glenmoore from 1952 to 1962. In the 1960s he was chairman of National Camping and the first Boy Scouts of Canada Camping Conference, as well as a participant and leader in national and international conferences and workshops. Throughout the 1960s he was a Scoutmaster, Venturer Advisor, and Rover Leader for the 1st Penetanguishene. He was an instrumental member of the Scout '68 Task Group in Ontario, at a time when many changes were taking place in Scouting programs and uniforms. In the 1970s he was a member and chairman of the World Training Committee and the Program Committee. Robbert was also involved with the African Training Committee to which he was a great asset, as he recognized the international differences and the need for variety in Scouting programs. He was involved with the World Organization of Scouting throughout Africa, in several South American countries, and in some of the poorest countries, like Kenya, Guatemala, and Indonesia.

Sea Scouts aboard Robbert's boat *Sea Flight*.

Robbert travelled beyond Georgian Bay with some of his Scouts for the 8th World Scout Jamboree at Niagara-on-the-Lake in 1955. He took

SCOUT LEADERS MAKE ROCHESTER STOPOVER—Robbert Hartog, Sea Scout-master of Toronto, Ont. (left), and Col. John Skinner Wilson, former head of International Scouting Bureau, native of London, (center) discuss 8th World Scout Jamboree on Rochester stop with Jack Stern, Scoutmaster of Rochester Tay House Troop 19, host to Scout visitors.

Sea Scouts in their navy blue uniforms sitting on top of *Sea Flight* at the World Scout Jamboree in Niagara on the Lake.

his Scouts by boat from their Collins Inlet campsite on Mill Lake, through Lakes Huron and Erie to Niagara, after first waiting out Hurricane Connie in the Windsor/Detroit area, and stopping in Rochester. From time to time, the propellers of the boat were lifted into the air because the waves were so large during the stormy weather. They eventually made it to the Jamboree and felt the blistering heat in their dark blue, long pant Sea Scout uniforms, joining 11,139 Scouts from 71 countries. Some of the international Scouts joined Robbert and his Sea Scouts aboard the *Sea Flight* for rides into the lake or in the locks of the Welland Canal. Not all went according to plan. On one trip the canal broke down and Robbert and the Scouts on board were stuck for 13 hours! Robbert enjoyed speaking to the international Scouts in the multiple languages he knew, including Dutch, French, German, English (he picked up a little bit of Spanish later in life). One troop from French Equatorial Africa travelled on the boat with Robbert and a couple of kids told off-colour jokes. No one else knew, because they were speaking French. They went on for a while and then Robbert turned and responded in French, much to the boys' embarrassment.

In 1957 Robbert took several Scouts with him to the 9th World Scout Jamboree in Sutton Park, England. This Jubilee Jamboree celebrated Scouting's 50th anniversary. As a special treat, Robbert arranged for the Scouts to have afternoon tea with his mother on their trip to Sutton Coalfield.

Twenty years later, Robbert was part of the Coordinating Committee for the Canadian Jamboree in Prince Edward Island, where 16,000 boys attended. "It was intended to be a large (and it was larger than anticipated) boy-centred (and such it was) event and was enthusiastically received by the Scout membership," Robbert said. "The fact that in general the enthusiasm at the end was as high as before the Jamboree indicates the success of this event. It is most heartening to note the reaction of the Scouts to the flexibility introduced, the way they behaved, the increasing friendliness displayed."

Robbert was recognized for his involvement with Scouting as early as 1949, when he was given a Long Service Medal. He would receive it again in 1954 and in 1959. In February 1949 he also received the Medal of Merit "For Good Service to Scouting." In 1959 he was awarded the Bar to Medal of Merit "For Continued Especially Good Service to Scouting." On June 22, 1970, Robbert was bestowed the highest recognition award in Scouting — the Silver Wolf. This award is given "For Service of the Most Exceptional Character to Scouting." As the citation outlined in recognizing Robbert's contributions to Scouting:

> Robbert Hartog is a person of prodigious energy, with a mind which is both incisive and perceptive. He brings to his associations a personality which, while frank and provocative, remains creative and stimulating. He is a person, who, in the fullest meaning of the words, is creative and stimulating. He is a person, who, in the fullest meaning of the words, is "in touch" — in touch with youth and their thinking, in touch with contemporary society, and in touch with the behavioural sciences. It is this blend of practised experience and erudition which has equipped Robbert Hartog to bring insight to many of the problems of Canadian Scouting. He has used these talents without stint. His services as a member of one committee after another have involved degrees of effort and commitment far exceeding those normally implied. These committees have included some of the most demanding assignments, with frequent and lengthy meetings, interspersed with extensive preparation. Robbert Hartog has been a key factor in the development and acceptance of the new concepts upon which the very future of Scouting is based. Robbert Hartog has made a great contribution to Scouting.

Robbert (third from the right) at a Jamboree planning meeting.

In 1981 Robbert was further recognized for his involvement when the World Organization of Scouting awarded him with the Bronze Wolf at the World Scout Conference in Dakar, Senegal. The medal acknowledged Robbert's services in international Scouting. In 75 years of Scouting, only 147 Bronze Wolf awards had been distributed throughout the world. People from all over the world who were familiar with Robbert's involvement recommended him for the award. He also became one of the earliest Baden Powell (B.P.) Fellows when he was awarded the fellowship in 1982. The fellowship, named after Lord Robert Baden Powell, the founder of Scouting, recognizes individuals for their contributions to the World Scout Foundation and provides lifetime association with the Scout movement and with business, government and Scouting leaders who share the same ideals. Robbert was also named a Scouts Canada Foundation Fellow.

Always Be Prepared

The Scout motto is "Be Prepared." Robbert became an expert in dealing with the unexpected. He often gave up his weekends and summer vacation to spend time on his boat with the Scouts. He was proud of all of his official honours, but he cherished his experiences with the Scouts most of all. Over the years Robbert had many wonderful, sometimes scary, other times comical, but all worthwhile experiences. Not a single boy was lost during the sometimes harrowing adventures, but many a man was born. Stories of these experiences are cherished by the generations of men who fondly recall their experiences with "Skip" Hartog.

Late one evening, Hudson Leavens (a Scout in the 81st Toronto Sea Scout Group) was fishing while camping with his troop. Suddenly he felt a sharp pain in the back of his leg. A fishhook was stuck. Robbert rushed him to the doctor in Little Current. As they sat together and waited, Hudson recalls that Robbert "talked to me more in those few hours than he did in the rest of my life." During another trip, a Scout was lost overnight while camping on an island playing a wide-area game. The boys were organized and set out in different directions to find the missing boy, but not before they divided up his things among them in case he did not come back, with one Scout saying, "I call his hatchet!" Robbert remained calm and had everything organized. They woke up at dawn and they set off in groups in different directions with orders to turn around in an hour. The Scouts used their compasses to eventually find the missing boy.

"Everything was meticulously planned, but you've got about 35 or 40 young boys running around. The plans usually fell apart and, of course,

everybody sort of realized that and we all sort of watched to see when the plan would unravel. Then we'd laugh. We thought it was pretty funny and we'd say, 'Well, there goes another one of his well-laid plans,' said Steve Glogowski (81st Toronto Sea Scout Group). Robbert would adjust; he would make another plan. Mac Phair (81st Toronto Sea Scout Group) said, "I think he fully expected it to happen ... He'd say, 'We'll do this plan and see what happens, but you know it will go wrong, and when it goes wrong we'll deal with that,'" Bill Moore (81st Toronto Sea Scout Group) admits, "That's why it was so much fun." Robbert's patience with various camping and boating disasters was tested over the years and he generally remained calm. If the Scouts crossed Robbert, however, they knew right away. If one of them did something to make him angry, he was exasperated, and there were consequences. He would let out a loud growl and he would be in a bad mood for a while.

The camp to which Robbert took the boys had become so popular that some of the Scouts were driven up in the "Green Giant," a green extended station wagon that Robbert had specially made to transport the Scouts. "He had the greatest things for Scouts. When we went to his camp we were busy all the time," Hudson recalled. "He would teach us how to cook our food, everything." Ralph Befort (former 1st Penetanguishene Scout and Venturer) remembered Robbert teaching them how to start a fire with birchbark, even if it was soaked. Robbert encouraged his boys to earn a number of badges. David Webster (Penetang/Midland Scouts) said Robbert "actually helped me get my Queen Scout when I was only 13 — that was quite an accomplishment." Doug Lorriman (81st Toronto Sea Scout Group) explained that a lot of the activities at the camp, such as games, compass-reading exercises, were aimed at helping the Scouts get merit badges. Many former Scouts recalled "Survival Day," when three or four boys were put on an island with a couple of matches, a hatchet, a drink of water, and a live chicken. Some boys refused to catch the chicken; others killed it, plucked it, and built a fire and a spit to have dinner that night. Robbert sent letters home to the parents of the Scouts to let them know how their sons had done at camp. He graded them on activities such as swimming. He assessed them with a letter grade and then marked improvements on notepapers. Robbert was very multi-generational, so he also became good friends with a number of the boys' parents.

In June 1957, Robbert and his Scouts' preparedness for survival was seriously tested. Robbert travelled with six Scouts from the 81st Toronto Scout Group on his 40-foot cruiser, *Sea Flight*, late on the evening

Young Scouts showing their catch on "Survival Day."

CABIN CRUISER SLICED BY FREIGHTER, SAVE 7

TORONTONIANS THROWN INTO GEORGIAN BAY

Special to The Star

Midland, June 22 — Seven Toronto persons escaped drowning last night after they were thrown into Georgian Bay when the freighter Quedoc rammed their 40-foot cabin cruiser.

Robert Hartog, 36, of Crescent Rd., owner of the cruiser, charged the freighter changed course at the last minute as the two vessels neared each other and sliced his cruiser toward the stern.

Taken to Midland

Mr. Hartog and his guests were picked up by a boat from the freighter and taken to Midland for treatment of cuts and bruises at St. Andrew's hospital.

Besides Mr. Hartog, they included Michael Phair, 23, of Glen Rd.; John Vernon, 17, of Edgedale Rd.; Larry Halliday, 18, of Astley Ave., and Evan Monkman, 17, William Moore, 17, and Robert Armstrong, 17, all of Douglas drive.

They were en route from Penetanguishene to Little Current for the week-end.

Capt. Munroe MacDonald of the Quedoc refused comment on the accident today, but Hartog admitted the captain disagreed with his version.

Hartog said his boat, Sea Flight, and the freighter were

ROBERT HARTOG
His Boat Rammed

of the 22nd. It was rare for them to travel at night, but that evening they were taking supplies to the campsite on the North Channel near Little Current. The Scouts on board included Mac Phair, John Vernon, Larry Halliday, Evan Monkman, William Moore, and Robert Armstrong, all from the 81st Toronto Sea Scout Group. The young men were between 17 and 23 years old. Larry was brushing his teeth and Bill and Mac went to bed for the night. They did not realize anything was wrong until they saw some lights and someone said, "Look at the boat!" The *Sea Flight* and *Quedoc*, a freighter, were approaching port to port. Then suddenly the freighter gave two whistles indicating that it was going to turn to port. Robbert said, "As soon as she started to turn, it was inevitable that she would run us down." The freighter rammed into Robbert's boat and part of the stern broke open. The vessel started to take on water. "By the rules I should have also turned to port when the freighter signalled her intention, but if I'd done so we would have been cut in two amidships," said Robbert. "So I turned to starboard and the bow of the freighter caught us near the stern." After the crash Robbert went up to the top deck and quickly began cutting life vests.

Robbert and the young men were soon in the waters of Georgian Bay. The current was moving in the opposite direction of the boat wake, causing the water to become choppy. Two of the youth, Bill Moore and Mac Phair, were in the stern of the cabin. "I can remember standing on the back of the cabin," Bill recalled. "We went out where the boat came in." Life jackets came floating by them because Robbert strategically stowed them in various places on the boat. "We couldn't get up into the main cabin," explained Mac. "The boat hitting our boat compressed the frame of the doorway that would get us back up, it was jammed and the stern was down and filling with water … The back part of the cabin was torn off." The freighter sent out a life raft and picked up Robbert and the Scouts. Captain Munro MacDonald of the *Quedoc* refused to comment on the accident to the press, but Robbert commented that the captain disagreed with his version of the freighter's last-minute change in course. In the end, Robbert pursued a legal process that proved that the freighter was at fault.

"One thing Robbert always had was a knack for walking into a room. He never demanded respect," said Ralph Befort. "He would just walk quietly and had an aura around him. When he would open his mouth people would just listen. The Boy Scouts would listen to him, even the troublemakers. They certainly respected Robbert as a leader because he had 'presence that demanded respect,' said Doug Lorriman. Robbert took on a lot of responsibility with young boys on his boat in the wilderness, but their respect for him made the trips enjoyable. "He always had time for the kids," said Ralph. "He was such a busy guy in his business, and was so successful, but he would take his boat for three weeks to a Boy Scout Jamboree in PEI." He could have taken this time with his friends, but he chose to do it with the Scouts. "Even though he was a big business man and a wise man, he was a solid father figure for many people," Ralph said. Sometimes the boys would let it slip and call him Dad because they got "that close to him," noted Rob Thorburn (81st Toronto Sea Scout Group). "He was your surrogate father when you were there." The boys had their own father figures, but they looked up to Robbert with respect similar to that they gave their fathers.

Robbert gave the Scouts respect and responsibility in return. Mac recalled meetings with Robbert at his house on Crescent Road in Rosedale. Robbert included the 12 to 14-year-olds in the decision making. They would even receive the meeting minutes. Larry Halliday remembered Robbert's "Court of Honour" meetings where the Scouts would make the decisions in a laissez-faire manner. He ran a participatory democracy. "Robbert was one of the first to treat us as adults," said Mac. "The thing that was fun for us all was that our parents would say don't do this or don't do that, but Robbert would let us do it and see how it turned out," reminisced Bill.

One trip, Robbert drove with six Scouts to Fort Lauderdale, Florida, in the Green Giant for a boat trip to the Bahamas. He typically drove like a European — he was a good driver, but he tended to speed. Petula Clark's "Downtown" was popular on the radio at that the time. "Somehow every time that came on the radio, it would be cranked right up. It didn't matter what time of night or who was sleeping, it would be cranked right up and the whole car would be singing with Petula Clark," remembers Doug. "When the song was over, the radio would be cranked down and everyone would go back to sleep." When the Scouts arrived in Fort Lauderdale there were small craft warnings because of high winds, so they could not leave the first day. On the second day the warning remained, but on the morning of the third day the warning was lifted for a time, so they boarded a Chris-Craft boat, which was much smaller than the *Sea Flight*, and set out on the water. Just after they left, the small craft warning was reissued. "We had to go across to the first island, which was Bimini. We got out there and we got into the Gulf Stream, and in the Gulf Stream the current was going north and the wind was coming from another direction. Then there was some kind of tide effect in a third direction and the waves were going into pyramids," explained Steve Glogowski. He recalled being sick over the stern of the boat because of the extreme rocking motion. "We got to Bimini and the place was deserted." There was a big hotel there but no one else was on the island because of the weather. Robbert and the Scouts were invited to the bar and the hotel had a band playing. "We had a ball," Steve recalled.

The next day they started across to the next island, but the wind was against them. They could see their destination, but they had to go around the island to get to the harbour. They got into something called the "Tongue of the Ocean." The Bahamas reef is 1,100 metres deep in sections. When the tide comes in the water piles up. The boat went up over the large waves and then would bang down, ringing the bell mounted on the boat. "I'm sitting there watching the shore and the waves are pounding on this corral, spraying all the way up and we're not moving," remembers Steve. "We're caught in this thing going up and down and up and down." Robbert was at the helm and began to rev up the engines and nothing happened. He called Steve over and said, "Would you go check the fuel tanks?" So Steve took a stick to the starboard tank and the stick sank to the bottom of the tank, which had only about one inch of fuel. He went to the portside tank and the stick sank in that tank as well. Steve said to Robbert, "There's about an inch left in each tank." Robbert said, "Okay, fine. Don't tell the other kids." He revved the engine up to full speed and finally they broke out of the waves and made it to the harbour. "There were a lot of close calls with Robbert," Steve said.

On one winter camping trip in Haliburton, Ontario, in minus 55 degree Fahrenheit weather, "we dug a hole through the ice and [Robbert] went for a swim," recalled Mac. "He said if we dug the hole he would swim. So, okay, we dug a hole and he did." After the trip the boys returned home with stories of how cold it was and how they almost froze. One parent called Robbert and said, "How can you expose my little boy to all of this terrible stuff?" Robbert replied, "Well if you don't like it then just don't send him to Scouts." Of course, that was the end of it, because all of the Scouts wanted to be a part of the adventures with Robbert.

David Webster recalled a canoe trip down the French River with Rob-bert during a Scout or Venture trip. Robbert wanted to shoot the rapids, but his canoe tipped. He lost money and credit cards, but he was most annoyed that everyone saw his spill. "He was great; he was a really good sport," David acknowledged. "He forced us all at least to our limits … He really brought out the best in people. He encouraged us all to do things that, given our own laziness and stuff, we probably would have never done."

When Robbert moved to Cambridge in the 1980s he continued his involvement with Scouting with a group at the Trinity Church in Galt. John Bell (a former Scout from the 81st Toronto Sea Scout Group) was the assistant Scoutmaster. Robbert enjoyed telling the story of when John was a Sea Scout junior leader, attending the camp near Little Current. One day he took a small outboard boat out to get supplies and groceries. Before leaving for the store he forgot to put the plug back into the boat after it was left to drain. He came back from the store and the lines on either end of the boat were there, but the boat had sunk. The Ontario Provincial Police came and took John back to the camp. Robbert met them on his boat, *Clytie*, and told John to "Get down here!" and he told the police he would tell him "what for." John remembers, "After the police left he laughed and he laughed and called me a stupid idiot, which I guess I was!"

When Robbert reached the age of 65 he decided to resign all Scout involvements and focus on other international tasks. He remained interested in Scouting and kept in contact with the World Scout Organization. He continued to make periodic trips to Geneva to meet with old contacts. Although he was no longer directly involved, he also continued to financially support the organization with personal contributions to the Scouts Canada Foundation.

Many of the Scouts first met Robbert when they were young, but their lives crossed paths with Robbert throughout their careers. Bruce Currie (113th Toronto Scout Group) met Robbert in the summer of 1941. That year, for the first time ever, the Rotary Club of the United States met outside of the United States, in Toronto at the Royal York Hotel. There were thousands who came by train to Union Station. Part of the welcoming committee was a group of Boy Scouts and their leaders. They would carry the passengers' baggage through the station and into the hotel and help them get checked in with the Rotary Club. Robbert was a Scout leader at Union Station and he met Bruce amid the chaos. Robbert introduced himself and told Bruce that when he decided to go from Cub Scout to Boy

Scout, he should come to Rosedale United Church, where Robbert was a leader. Bruce joined the 113th Toronto Scout Group and continued to keep in touch with Robbert as he started to build his company. Robbert first asked Bruce to work as a driver at his plant in Ajax and later, when the factory moved to Midland, he asked Bruce to come with him. Bruce became vice-president of marketing for Waltec Enterprises Ltd. and he continued the long-standing friendship with Robbert that had begun when he was a youth.

A number of Robbert's Scouts have similar stories of how they continued their relationship with him. It is astounding how many leaders in the community and long-time friends of Robbert were former Scouts. Hudson Leavens started working for Robbert in Midland in 1973. He was general manager for 14 years and the two became close friends. Robbert hired David Webster in 1976. He is the current CEO and CFO of Baytech Plastics, formerly Waltec Plastics. "He was just a real generous guy," said David. "He was definitely my mentor, no question about it … from Scouting right into the business. I felt quite honoured that he hired me and searched me out and then out of the 25 people that he chose at the end, I was one of those. I was rather proud." Scouts such as David, Hudson, Ralph Befort, Jim Worts and others were also philanthropically involved in Midland and often worked with Robbert on various campaigns for the Wye Marsh, the hospital, and other endeavours. Many more stayed in touch with him over the years. A number of his friends who were invited on his boating trips in the summer were former Scouts. John Bell (who became a prominent Canadian business leader and who served as CEO of a number of companies as well as being a leading philanthropist) said that Robbert would have to choose you as a friend after Scouts, and if you were invited

Robbert (sixth from the left) and his former Scouts at a Boys' Night Out gathering.

Boys' Night Out at the Wellington Brewery. Robbert (second row, third from the left) is reunited with his former Scouts.

on a boating trip that was a big deal, because that is how Robbert chose to socialize with people. Some of his Scouts became leaders themselves once they were old enough. When Robbert moved to Midland, for example, Larry Halliday and a couple of other Scouts took over troops in Toronto.

The Scouts who grew up together kept in touch with each other, as well as with Robbert. Boys' Night Out (also known as the Rosedale Commando) has existed since 1963. Former Scouts started to get together when the young men graduated from university. It used to go from 5 p.m. to the early hours of the morning, but in later years the night only went until about 9 p.m. Robbert went to a Boys' Night Out with the old Scouts a few years ago. That year they rented the top floor of a tavern called the Bow and Arrow on Yonge Street in Toronto. Everyone puts in some money to cover food and drinks, but there is always some left over, so a draw is made and the winner gets to give the leftover money to the charity of his choice. Jim Worts (113th Toronto Scout Group) recalled Robbert saying he would not attend again. "I guess he just wanted to see what these crazy Scouts do." There have been a number of get-togethers over the years, giving Robbert and his Scouts a chance to reminisce and catch up.

On January 30, 1999, a number of Robbert's former Scouts organized the "Great Reunion." Robbert wrote Hudson, thanking him for his participation in the gathering:

Robbert (fourth from the right)
with his former Scouts.

I know that most youth leaders would love to see what happened 25, 30, 40, or 50 years later, when the young people of the past have become mature (more mature?). You gave me that privilege and at the same time I had the pleasure of meeting those who you knew so well in your youth. It is a tribute to Scouting that so many turned up — and it was, once more, proof that the main influence in Scouting — comes from the other Scouts.

The men gave Robbert a beautiful paddle as a thank-you gift, which he kept in a place of honour in his home, but Robbert said, "The best memento is the pleasure of seeing you all."

Dana Taylor (81st Toronto Sea Scout Group) came across Robbert's contact information almost four decades after being a Scout under his leadership in the early 1960s. He wrote a letter to Robbert with friendly recollections of times past. "The appreciation I now have for the wilderness I attribute to these early camping and Scouting days," he said. "My purpose in writing was to remember myself to you and to do something that I would never have thought to do properly as a youth. I thank you for the opportunity of a lifetime and the great memories that have lasted throughout." Robbert replied, "At this, in a somewhat more reflective life cycle, it is very nice to hear from the past — and to learn that some efforts were appreciated." Dana and Robbert eventually reunited over cookies and cola at Robbert's home in Perkinsfield on April 1, 2007. Dana wanted to visit Robbert if only because he had remembered him after all of that time and distance. Robbert's parting comment at the door was "Shall we do this again in another 45 years?" Dana said he would stick around if Robbert would. In a follow-up letter, Dana wrote, "However dissimilar and different our paths have been I regard you as an important mentor in my life, and you continue to be a purposeful example for me of how to stay involved in the world around us."

David Webster once asked Robbert if there was anything else he might want to do with his life. Robbert said, "From time to time I have thought that maybe I would have rather been a professor." David reassured him,

"You have the best of both worlds, you have been teaching us all the time." Robbert influenced his Scouts in a unique way. Many of them continued their interest in the Canadian wilderness, with a few joining him on canoe trips in northern Canada. Rob Thorburn said, "A lot of these things that Hartog did meant a lot to us. I would say that my boating on Georgian Bay, which has been really extensive since I was in my 20s, going up and down the coast of Georgian Bay, was really triggered by Robbert Hartog. It was so fun, and so interesting and so fabulous that we sort of carried on." Robbert's mentoring and the example he set for the boys inspired them to give back to society. "He had an amazing impact on an enormously wide part of society that he touched," reflected Mac Phair. "There are unique people, special, whatever you want to call them and he was one. I've never met anyone like him. The impact in a positive way of such a huge, wide group of people, quite disparate people from all kinds of walks of life.

Robbert proudly shows off the paddle he was given from the Scouts.

He accepted people for what they were." Robbert treated the boys as individuals and respected their achievements. Through his example he taught the value of community work and the virtues of integrity and trustworthiness. "We were challenged to surmount obstacles and hardships with our ingenuity and endurance," Steve Glogowski explained. "All of these things have formed a link between those of us who had the privilege of growing up with Robbert, and have left an indelible mark on our lives."

Robbert's intellect and leadership was contagious to those whom he mentored. The Scouts had the opportunity to learn from Robbert's example, and they cherished their adventures with him; his leadership made him an unforgettable father figure. As youths, the Scouts were unaware of Robbert's business achievements and his extensive involvement in the community; only when they were older could they truly grasp the context of his accomplishments. Many years have passed since the nights by the campfire in ghastly canvas army surplus tents, or the wild boating adventures. But to the Scouts, Robbert will always be "Skip" Hartog.

CHAPTER SEVEN

A Love of the Canadian Wilderness

Canoeing and boating allowed Robbert Hartog to see and experience first-hand the Canadian wilderness. He understood the importance of protecting nature as he travelled to remote lands, saw polar bears, seals, and moose in their environment, and paddled pristine waters. After seeing the beauty of the rivers and the landscape, he was linked to the land and geography of Canada. His passion for nature, paired with his desire to give back to conservation, led to his support of the World Wildlife Fund (WWF) in Canada and the Wye Marsh Wildlife Centre.

World Wildlife Fund

In 1973 Robbert joined "The 1001: A Nature Trust." The members of the trust are contributors to the WWF whose support helps the organization achieve its mission and further the environmental cause at the highest levels. There are sparse records of Robbert's involvement with the WWF in the early to mid-1970s, but it is evident that by the 1980s he was a loyal annual supporter. Soon after becoming executive director of World Wildlife Fund Canada in 1978, Monte Hummel was introduced to Robbert at a board of directors meeting. According to Monte, they got about two sentences into their conversation

Robbert was a firm believer in the importance of preserving the wetlands at the Wye Marsh.

and he realized, "There's only one guy in this room who's paddled more rivers in northern Ontario, who's paddled more rivers than me, and it's this guy." Soon after, the two canoe enthusiasts enjoyed a kind of "kindred spirit" relationship. Robbert remained on the WWF board of directors until the mid-1990s. His enthusiasm for the organization, paired with his trust and respect for Monte (who became president of the WWF and is now president emeritus), fuelled his involvement.

The WWF, a non-governmental organization, was founded in 1961 (1967 in Canada) to save threatened wildlife and their natural environments around the world. According to its 2008 annual report, WWF is one of the largest multinational organizations around the world. Its mission is "To stop the degradation of the planet's natural environment and to build a future in which humans live in harmony with nature, by: conserving the world's biological diversity; ensuring that the use of renewable natural resources is sustainable; and promoting the reduction of pollution and wasteful consumption." In Canada specifically, WWF works coast to coast to protect ecosystems, create more sustainable fisheries and forestry operations, and tackle vital issues like fresh water and climate change. It has approximately five million supporters worldwide, most of whom are regular donors. Their contributions make up the majority of the organization's overall budget.

Robbert was a faithful, anonymous donor, but more than that, he contributed wise counsel on a variety of WWF endeavours. He became a confidant to Monte, who could not recollect much rhyme or reason to Robbert's support in the early years, apart from the fact that it was very generous and substantial for someone whom he would see once a year at a general meeting. Over the years, Monte recognized that "this man was really not only a strong financial supporter and fellow traveller, but he really had a wonderful mind, a strategic mind, [he was] a really good board member." Monte started to encounter what he called "the wisdom of Robbert Hartog" when WWF worked to protect the endangered beluga population in the Saguenay Fjord, where the Saguenay River tumbles down into the St. Lawrence River. In the late 1980s, Robbert took a vacation on his boat from Penetanguishene out through the Great Lakes, past Kingston, down the St. Lawrence and to Newfoundland. He went right by the Saguenay Fjord.

Monte approached Robbert and asked him for a major financial contribution to the project. A few days later, a substantial cheque arrived in the mail. Once Robbert started giving at this higher level, Monte started to meet with him and give him progress reports. At this point the WWF benefited from Robbert's advice. According to Monte, Robbert would "read whatever we would send him, he thought about it, and always had two or three really interesting points that were off the wall or contrary." They were not the usual "keep it up, it all looks great to me." "He would say, 'Be careful about this' or 'This looks like a tough project unless you can get x or y.'" There is the saying, "If you want money, ask for advice." Monte's corollary is, "If you ever wanted advice, try asking for money." With Robbert it was a little bit of both. This advice came with the best of intentions. In his experience with Robbert, Monte knew he was "a thoughtful person, not soft, but demanding. He would give someone enough rope to prove himself or not. He liked things spelled out. He was rigorous about things."

Throughout the 1990s Robbert made donations to various WWF projects, including the Nature of Tomorrow Campaign, in 1997. In 1998 he made a pledge to the "Northern Futures" program, which supported the Wildlife Toxicology Data Collection work. Robbert also brought WWF to the attention of Fairfax Financial when he was on the company's Donation Committee. In the 1990s, WWF ran its Endangered Spaces Campaign. This project established over 1,000 new parks and protected areas in Canada and more than doubled the protected area in the country. A month after its successful conclusion in 2001, Monte was enthusiastic about a new campaign he described as "very different than any other, not a traditional wilderness campaign with posters and getting southern people to write to ministers saying 'protect this pretty place!'"

The Central Barrens, in the Canadian Arctic, is one of the few untouched places left in the world: 50 million acres of intact, wild natural habitat. The Aboriginal people call it "The Place Where God Began." In 2001, the WWF started a campaign to extend conservation in the heart of this natural area, to reach the 13.8 million-acre Thelon Wildlife Sanctuary. During the Endangered Spaces Campaign Alex Hall, a famed canoe guide in the central Arctic, and David Pelly, well-known author, approached Monte with the project. David and Alex had a dream of linking up two of the largest protected areas in the country: the Thelon Wildlife Sanctuary that spans Nunavut and the Northwest Territories, and the Queen Maud Gulf Migratory Bird Sanctuary in Nunavut. They planned to work in co-operation and collaboration with the native peoples of the lands: the Dene (who relate to the part of the sanctuary in the Northwest Territories) and the Inuit (who relate to the part of the sanctuary in Nunavut and the Queen Maud). If successful, this would mean 50 million

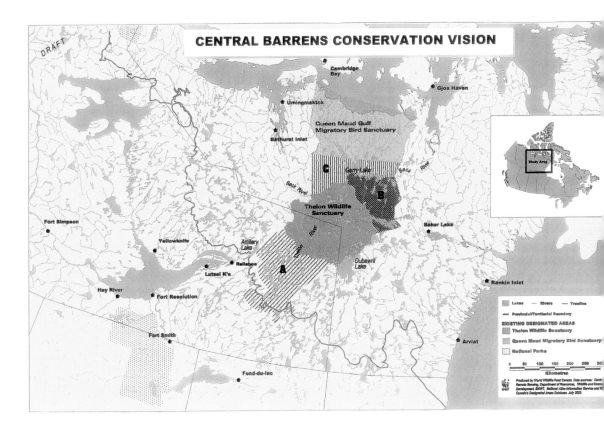

CENTRAL BARRENS CONSERVATION VISION

A map outlining the objectives of the Central Barrens project.

acres of protected lands up the spine of Canada — no roads, no communities, just the magnificent Central Barrens of northern Canada. There are caribou calving areas all through the area. Migratory herds move back and forth across the area and they have traditionally been hunted from the southwest by the Dene and hunted by the Inuit from the northeast. This meant that the two cultures would meet in this part of the country, but not always on a friendly basis.

To make the Central Barrens project a reality, Monte needed a short list of loyal financial supporters. It was to be a 3 to 5-year project, but very high risk, with no certainty of success. Monte knew, "If we did succeed, the conservation prize at the end is phenomenal — the largest in the country, a beautiful, wild part of the country." He came up with a short list of six people whom he believed "would have the philanthropic guts to take this on and take a flyer, bet on me, because I was leading the project. Who has got enough faith in me to take a shot at this? Who would put a quarter of a million into this over the next 3 to 5 years and if it didn't succeed, would not feel like it was a total waste of time because it was understood from the beginning that this was a high-risk project."

"Robbert was on my list," said Monte. He sent him the proposal, and Robbert was one of the first people that said, "Count me in." For the next seven years he contributed annually to what he called "the big project." Robbert suspected from the beginning that 3 to 5 years was not enough. He thought that it would take longer and he was right. Once a year Monte would meet with Robbert at the Jolly Miller, at the Miller Tavern on Yonge Street in Toronto. Robbert would eat the same thing every time, and Monte would roll out the maps and give him a progress report. Two days later, Robbert's cheque to support the project would arrive in the mail.

Early in 2001 Monte offered Robbert the opportunity to canoe the Arctic on a personally guided trip with the legendary Alex Hall. This was "by invitation only," for a handful of main donors to the Central Barrens project. The trip would take them to the expansive wild to see it first-hand by canoe. Robbert was intrigued by the offer. He said, "On one hand, an Arctic canoe trip — one last one! — in [August] 2002 has a lot of attractions … However, after a few nights, I came to the conclusion that it would be stupid, for an (as I will be in 2002) 83-year-old person to go on such a trip. It would be unfair to put such a risk — with the other participants. Therefore (and this is final with regards), I have decided that I should not participate in this alluring canoeing adventure." Monte understood, but was disappointed, as he admitted to Robbert that it was one of his secret hopes to wield a paddle with him someday. "I have long envied and admired your past wilderness experiences," he said to Robbert, "and your obvious deep feeling for healthy lands and waters — a passion I share."

In 2007 the Central Barrens project succeeded, achieving the largest land withdrawal for conservation in Canadian history, all the way from Great Slave Lake out to the Thelon. On the Northwest Territories side it was a resounding success, as both the Northwest Territories and Nunavut approved the Thelon Wildlife Sanctuary Management Plan, which included special management areas. The Nunavut side was more problematic, as the Inuit were very pro-development and mines appeared to be more important than the protection of the calving areas of the caribou (the most important land-based species in the Arctic). Robbert coined the term "the caribou economy," as he recognized that the caribou had become the lightning rod for the whole Central Barrens project.

On May 18, 2007, philanthropist Glen Davis, another major supporter of the Central Barrens project, was murdered in the underground parking lot of the WWF building in Toronto. This came as a huge shock to everyone at WWF, including Robbert. He knew Glen from WWF functions and he understood that Glen was a major donor to the project. Robbert wrote a letter to Monte the following week, saying, "I do not know if Glen's portion for 2007 has been paid, but if not, let me know and I will pay the missing amount, in his name, so that the project can successfully end, as it should [and] as he would have liked to see it end." Truly thankful for the extraordinary offer, Monte replied, "Robbert, thank you, but that isn't going to be necessary, as Glen has [left] two years funding for this project with us." In making such an offer, Robbert demonstrated an unwavering commitment above and beyond his already substantial monetary support.

WWF's work in the Canadian north pressed on to maintain "the caribou economy." Robbert was instrumental in this project and he stood by Monte for its duration. He said to Monte, "I had rationalized in my mind that, even if unsuccessful, our 'coup' was well worth trying. Now that there is a successful ending, it has been (thanks to your efforts) more than worthwhile." Throughout the journey, Robbert reassured Monte, "As far as this fascinating project is concerned, I am committed for the duration." Robbert enjoyed playing what he called "a small, supporting role" in a "most challenging adventure." Robbert's passion for nature and the Canadian wilderness endured throughout his life, and while his canoeing days may have been over, Robbert poetically remarked, "I have not been able to forget the North."

The Wye Marsh Wildlife Centre

Robbert's passion for the Canadian wilderness reached to the far north, but he was also aware of the need for conservation and preservation in his own community. His real appreciation for nature was exemplified with his beautiful Perkinsfield property, where he had the wetland designated and protected. For more than two decades, Robbert was an avid supporter of the Wye Marsh Wildlife Centre, located in Tay Township, just south of the Town of Midland. Executive director of the Board of the Wye Marsh, Laurie Schutt, explained, "He saw the Marsh as his small example of nature that he could nourish locally when he couldn't get to the broader expanses across Canada."

The Wye Marsh, situated in the environmentally endowed location known as the Wye Valley, opened in 1969 as a wildlife interpretation centre for the general public to learn about the natural environment. At this time the Centre was a federal nature reserve, operated by Environment Canada. Several small properties were subsequently added to the wildlife

On the occasion of his 80th birthday, the friends of the Wye Marsh recognized Robbert as an honorary life member.

area, for a total block of 3,000 acres of wetlands and forest. During the first 15 years that it was operational, almost a half a million visitors had the chance to learn an appreciation for their local environment.

In 1973 Bob Whittam, then the executive director of the Board of the Wye Marsh, received a call from Robbert's secretary, asking for a placement for his niece, Beatrice Brom (formerly Mansell), who was studying biology. "Hartog speaking!" exclaimed Robbert as he answered a call from Bob. "Thanks for calling back. I just wanted to know if there would be a volunteer position for my niece, who is coming over from Holland in a few weeks. She would like to gain some experience in environmental education at the Wye Marsh." Bob said this was the first time that he could remember hearing the familiar and helpful voice "which would often be called upon and always available for advice." Beatrice came to the Wye Marsh for a four-month internship. She recalled that Robbert "organized a canoe trip for me and some women friends with their daughters. All of his friends were amazed: who had been able to make Robbert take women on a canoe trip??...I accepted, and only later realized what a very special event this had been." Robbert let Beatrice stay at his house in Midland and drive his Jeep at her convenience — "all things that he never let anyone do," she said. "I felt accepted by him, loved in an uncomplicated way…We didn't speak very much about personal things, but always had things to chat about. We shared our love for nature, love for the outdoors and for hiking."

After this initial contact, Robbert subsequently became interested in joining the board of directors. His business acumen as well as his astounding biological knowledge made him a valuable board member when he joined the Board of Directors of the Wye Marsh in 1985. Throughout his years on the board, Robbert attracted a number of strong business contacts. Bob Whittam recalled that he was "not only a great beneficiary, but a strong businessman that helped deal with the transition to a non-profit organization." In 1997, Robbert was on the Audit Committee, which he chaired in 1999. He even came to a meeting with sandwiches in hand for the committee to munch on. In 1998 he was given a Service Recognition Award from the board of directors.

In April 1985, when Robbert first joined the board, federal government cutbacks threatened to close the Wye Marsh Wildlife Centre and four sister centres were set to close. The cutbacks would eliminate the wildlife research programs conducted by the centres, including the monitoring of toxic chemicals in the Great Lakes. To save the centre, Robbert and a local naturalist club got involved because they saw the possibilities of the facility and the need to have a centre focused on environmental education. Robbert encouraged Doug Lewis (then the Member of Parliament for Simcoe-North) to take up the issue and Doug drew up contractual agreements and a lawyer's agreement with the government. Robbert assessed the problem saying, "I do NOT think that one should base any strategy on trying to change the minds of the authorities completely (and have them revert to pre-1984). It is not easy for politicians (and indeed all humans) to about-face completely. Moreover, there is such a strong desire in Ottawa to 'reduce the deficit' that appeals on how other savings are easier to accomplish fall on nearly deaf ears." He thought a workable plan should a) "Reduce expenses by say 20 to 40 per cent (depending on what is the absolute minimum required to subsist)"; b) "Get another authority (province?) to share a bit of the load"; and c) the most important measure: "Get private money… to support part of this (to more than a nominal amount), showing that the people are willing to 'put their money where their mouth is,' as well as providing a part privatization." Robbert admitted that these were not his original thoughts, but he said, "I have stolen many from what I have heard or read!" In October 1985 Robbert was asked to join an advisory task force and he agreed, saying, "My hope is that we will be able to do things one of these days and not find more reasons for further studies and delays. To quote a famous economist: 'In the long run, when we are all dead, further information might be useful.'"

Ultimately the supporters of the Wye Marsh secured bridge financing to keep the Centre open. Doug Lewis attributed this success to "a very strong board" and Robbert's leadership. "The government felt that a lot of things done by the federal government could be better done by individuals in the area with an interest, having a hands-on operation's role, than by running the thing as something the federal government did." This

Swans leading Marsh visitors through the wetlands.

"devolution" process started small, with facilities like the Wye Marsh, and eventually the government extended this model to PetroCan and Air Canada. The Wye Marsh was one of the first ventures of this kind and was a learning experience for the government and the operation. Robbert and Doug did not see eye to eye on partisan politics, but, as Doug noted, Robbert "never let politics enter into our relationship or what we were trying to do together. I tried to do the same, but it was because of the way he conducted himself that I said, 'Well, he's keeping politics out of that. So will I.'"

In 1986, the operations were turned over to the Friends of the Wye Marsh, who entered into a lease agreement with the federal government and ran the centre as a registered non-profit corporation. "We don't get a penny from the government, but we lease with the federal government, we pay $1 a year and I apply for a land-lease permit," Laurie Schutt (executive director of the Wye Marsh) explained. In Robbert's opinion, the Wye Marsh is better run when it is in the hands of local people.

As part of its mandate, the Wye Marsh offers a variety of interpretation programs for students and the general public to encourage a deeper appreciation and understanding of the environment and its resources, hoping "to spark a commitment to conserving wetlands, woodlands, and wildlife by creating exciting learning opportunities in a natural setting." The Friends of the Wye Marsh describe it as "an ecological jewel to be preserved at all costs." As a result, it has become an integral part of the local community and of the Canadian conservation community.

In 1988, the Wye Marsh joined a national restoration effort to reintroduce the Trumpeter swan to its native habitat. Each year, staff and volunteers from the Wye Marsh Wildlife Centre monitor approximately one-third of the Ontario Trumpeter swan population. Some 350 years ago the Trumpeter swan was a common sight in the Wye Valley. Since then, habitat loss and overhunting completely eliminated the species from eastern Canada. This high-profile program became a signature for the Wye Marsh. Robbert was on the Trumpeter Swan Reintroduction Committee in the late 1980s into the 1990s. His savvy business demeanour convinced Scott Paper to work with the Wye and donate $50,000 annually for three years, with Robbert being "largely responsible for the success of the program."

In 2000, Hudson Leavens came up with the idea to permanently honour the swan in a high-profile place in Midland's Waterfront Park, over-looking Georgian Bay. This was a major fundraising and awareness project for the Wye Marsh. In 2001 an impressive sculpture was completed as a

Trumpeter Swans playing in the wetlands.

symbol of the success of the Trumpeter swan program. Designed by local artist Ron Hunt, a former KIL employee, it is made out of mirror-finish stainless steel and towers over the waterfront at 25 feet tall, with a 25-foot wingspan. The sculpture was a co-operative project of the Friends of the Wye Marsh, the Town of Midland, and Kindred Industries, which supplied the material. Robbert, of course, was instrumental in securing Kindred's involvement.

The Trumpeter Swan sculpture looks out over Midland's waterfront.

In July 2001, Laurie Schutt became the executive director of the Wye Marsh board. "When I was hired," she said, "they kind of sugar-coated the financial situation and it was much worse than I anticipated." The Wye is complicated, as a non-profit facility without core funding. Six weeks after Laurie was hired, she had to present a budget to the board on which Robbert had sat since 1985. She had heard stories about him in the community, "about him being a wizard with figures and how you couldn't get anything over him." She admitted being intimi-dated and said, "I was shaking in my boots" in preparation for the meeting. She presented spreadsheets done for each department. Robbert went through the sheets quickly and said, "So you think in six months we'll be here, in a year this is where we're going to be ... ." He went through 12 spreadsheets in 30 seconds and had the bottom line instantly. Astonished, Laurie wondered, "Now what do I say to him?" He criticized the budget to death and she had to redo it, but within her first month on the job Robbert sent a contribution to the Wye Marsh. She explained that it was "typical Robbert Hartog letterhead, confidential, cheque inside to help cover the deficit I inherited, just signed, Robbert." This was a normal occurrence, as Laurie explained: "The Marsh always had financial difficulties, but Rob-bert was always in the background to bail it out if need be."

Laurie realized that it would take time for Robbert to warm up to her as a woman in a position of authority. In time, however, "instead of being the brusque, critical man sitting there, a man of very few words, he started to tease me. There was a change and then I was in." She speculates that she simply had to prove herself as an executive. After a couple of years, when she had earned his respect, he provided her with advice, knowing that she would take what he said to heart and act in the best interest of the Marsh. In 2004 he wrote, "Over the years, I have learned that one needs a solid financial plan, before one can think of how to get the money. Once we can agree on such a plan, we can look at fundraising to get there ... I realize that it looks at times like a Catch-22: we are in a deficit position

The extensive, lush wetlands of the Wye Marsh.

and need money to get out of the bind. While I agree that survival is the first requirement I believe we should also be working on a second front. What would bring us to a new, higher- core financially sustaining level?" Robbert admitted that he often rehashed things in his mind, such as troubles at the Wye Marsh, between the hours of 2 a.m. and 4 a.m.

Laurie and Robbert's greatest satisfaction came in 2004, when the Marsh earned a surplus with a stable economic plan and Robbert no longer had to write cheques for the centre. They were able to focus on where the Marsh should go and how to make it a sustainable facility. However, trouble came in 2006 when the Auditor General came down on Canadian Wildlife Services and Laurie's key contacts left their positions. "All of a sudden the contacts were gone and nothing was ever put in writing," Laurie said. She was to "cease and desist all activities that contravene the wildlife activities … I'm not even allowed to drive anything, so you can't even drive in the road, I'm not allowed to cut grass, not allowed to plant a tree." At that time, she lamented, "I might as well shut down." The then-acting regional director for Ontario replied, "We don't care." She informed Robbert of the problems and he said, "I've been itching for a fight." This piqued his interest. Robbert was ready to take on the government on this issue because he always saw the possibilities for the Wye Marsh. He devoted his efforts towards getting the government to loosen the purse strings or change the designation on the centre. He thought the government should let the Wye do as they pleased, as long as they were not harming the environment. A new trust relationship needed to be established. Robbert worked diligently on this and three proposals to the government were drawn up:

1) Give the Wye Marsh to the Friends of the Wye Marsh,
2) Work with the board, take the designation off, and contribute financially to get the building up to snuff, or
3) Work together to come up with a plan for where we could be five years from now.

So far, the government has ignored the proposals and the Wye Marsh, but Robbert always encouraged Laurie to push on: "If they're not going to say no then we just keep going…We can win this."

Laurie explained that the centre had big plans — a mini-wetland in the parking lot, food facilities in the building, and new technology in a revamped building. She said, "Robbert could see this, he could see the potential, and he could see the growth coming, but we needed an influx of cash (He had already said, this project will go; he would finance it basically. He didn't say he would, but the way he worked, it was going to happen regardless)." Robbert was frustrated, but his attitude was "Let's solve it, let's come up with a solution." In 2005 Robbert decided to resign from the board of directors, but Laurie convinced him to stay on for one more year. In the following years they continued to deal with government issues and she no longer had to ask him to remain on the board.

Robbert remained committed in his support for the Marsh. While the troubles with the government continued, he reflected on the state of affairs in November 2006, saying, "My father, who had a very common sense approach to business would say, 'This is a very dangerous period.' His opinion was that if things are difficult, everyone is careful, but when good times prevail — that is the time that one can become careless." Robbert remained vigilant, but he was very pleased with the Marsh's deserved successes. At an audit meeting at the end of 2007, the board learned that the past fiscal year was the first time revenues hit one million dollars and the centre had a surplus for the third year in a row. Robbert sat there and asked a few blunt questions. At the end of it, his only word was "Finally." According to Laurie, "You could tell he was absolutely tickled."

In 2004 the Wye Marsh had an event that featured canoeing the wetlands. Laurie believed this was the last time Robbert, who was getting frail, was in a canoe. Robbert's involvement with the wildlife centre fit many of the key things that drove him in life — his love for nature, canoeing, boating, and Canadian wilderness. These passions, combined with Robbert's belief in the value of the Wye Marsh facility, made him keep up the fight for its existence. According to Colin Harper, current president of the Wye Marsh, "The Wye wouldn't be here without him."

The Wye Marsh is able to offer programs like canoe trips for visitors to the wetlands with the support of Robbert over the years.

CHAPTER EIGHT

Anonymous Benefactor

When Robbert walked down the streets of Midland, most residents would not have recognized him. He was not stopped and thanked for his contributions to the community; rather, he walked about the town, much like any other citizen — known only by friends and acquaintances. Of them, few knew the extent of his charitable work. Robbert demanded that every donation he made was to remain "strictly anonymous." For this, he was known among charity organizers and capital campaign volunteers as "Mr. Anonymous."

Robbert received provincial and national awards for his service, including the Order of Canada, which he received in 1985 and a Bicentennial Medal from the Province of Ontario in recognition for his community contributions in 1984. The volunteer sector and fundraisers in the community were well aware of Robbert's far-reaching involvement. He spread his advice and donations to organizations large and small. The charities he chose to be involved with were varied: from the local hospital to the industrial park, from community living for people with exceptionalities to the United Church, and from a battered women's shelter to psychiatric support

Downtown Midland, Ontario; Robbert's adopted homeland.

One of the many traces of Robbert's anonymous generosity in Midland.

programs. All of these organizations provide support to the community. He was involved with them because he believed in the people running these organizations and because he believed in what the charities contributed. The extent of Robbert's charitable work in Midland and throughout the world may never be fully understood. Throughout his life he remained private and anonymous. However, he left traces of his involvement in his records and he left his mark on those with whom he worked. From these leads we can begin to understand his contributions to his community.

Huronia District Hospital

Robbert joined the Huronia District Hospital board in 1986 and it was clear "that Robbert was one of strong opinion and incredible leadership," said Arnold DeCarli, former chairman of the hospital. In the mid-1980s a Hospital Foundation was needed, with a separate corporation and board of directors, to fundraise and manage funds. Arnold and Robbert were the first directors of the Huronia District Hospital Foundation, founded on April 8, 1988. Together they developed a two-fold mandate focused on the capital needs of the hospital. First, they provided a future-oriented strategy which was independent of the operations of the hospital and directed by different individuals. Second, they separated any capital money from government directive, setting up a mechanism where the government could not divert capital funds into the operations of the hospital.

In 1988, Robbert and Arnold co-chaired a $2.8 million capital campaign, "No Better Time, No Better Cause." At the time Robbert was treasurer and Arnold was chairman. According to Laurene Sibley, the director of development for the Hospital Foundation since 1998, it "was the first real hospital campaign that was done at that kind of scale in our community." Robbert said he would chair the campaign if Arnold did it with him, not because he needed the help but, Arnold recalled, "That's just the way he wanted it." The 1988 campaign provided for improvement and expansion of the emergency department, opened a new

The Huronia District Hospital in Midland.

obstetrics area and moved laboratory services to a larger location. A new addition to the building housed these departments. When the hospital opened in 1976, a wing remained unfinished until funds from the capital campaign allowed its completion. Robbert's vision for the campaign turned into leadership to engage industry in supporting regional health. As a business leader in the community, Robbert ensured that his companies provided leadership to the campaign in order to set the pace for other major local industries to get involved. This early campaign set the fundraising bar for the current initiatives.

Through this experience, Arnold learned Robbert's "very forthright" fundraising technique. It was about personal leadership, both from making the kind of financial commitment that one could make to a campaign, whatever your ability, and expecting the same of the people upon whom you were calling. Robbert "was not shy in asking for big numbers from people, but he had a knowledge and experience that told him that this was correct."

Arnold DeCarli explained that the hospital sector was always under stress. "From an operational aspect of the hospital, Robbert brought an increased discipline to the financial aspects of the hospital," he observed. "When Robbert was around you felt very secure in his professionalism and his wisdom, and his vast experience. He was very good at putting things into perspective." As a young chairman he found Robbert to be a mentor for him. Over the years, the two became close through their work at the hospital and Arnold remembered a genuine and sincere relationship with Robbert. "He had an impact on absolutely everybody that he dealt with … Not only did Robbert make his own contribution, but he made your contribution better. He inspired you to bring more than you thought you were ready to bring, or capable of bringing, to meetings and to arguments. I think he taught me to think even more outside the box than I did."

Robbert "provided the leadership to put the hospital on a different footing. The whole concept of beginning a Foundation to guide the fundraising efforts of the hospital long into the future was something he was extraordinarily keen about." When Robbert retired from the board of the Foundation in 1994, he continued to attend the general membership meetings and he never failed to speak at the meetings, not gratuitously, but with a point. He kept people focused. Arnold was impressed that Robbert's "ability and his connections across the country gave him … incredible insight to the broad workings of health care and hospitals."

In 2005, Robbert joined the Huronia Hospitals Foundation
pre-campaign planning team. He was usually the first volunteer present
at the 7:30 a.m. meetings. He was on the Advisory Committee for the
$6 million capital campaign and at Robbert's suggestion, Arnold chaired
the leadership gift section of that campaign. The "Our Best Care"
campaign was aimed at improving the emergency department, helping
rehabilitation at the Penetanguishene hospital, and improving digital
imaging efficiency. According to Laurene, the "Our Best Care" title words
personally come from Robbert. She explained that Robbert wanted the
best hospital and the best health care in Midland. "He never gave me some
story about why he wanted to join the hospitals. All he ever really talked
about was [that] his personal commitment to the hospital revolved
around making sure it was the 'best.' And he used that word all the time."
Not only did Robbert personally donate to the campaign (he informed
Arnold of his donation in 2006, saying, "I would like to make your life
easy!" This would mean one less call for Arnold to make), but Fairfax
Financial also made a contribution in his name.

Robbert supported both Huronia District Hospital and the
Penetanguishene hospital and was a proponent of bringing the two
hospitals together. In the 1990s the hospitals joined the North Simcoe
Hospital Alliance and suggested that the Foundation become a joint
Foundation. Robbert supported this. After the alliance formed, the hospitals
had one Foundation for two corporations called Huronia Hospitals
Foundation. The hospitals united, as did the fundraising initiatives. After
the "Our Best Care" campaign, the Huronia District Hospital Board
recommended that the hospital become a Catholic hospital and amalgamate
with the Penetanguishine hospital. This was a financially based recommenda-
tion for government funding. Robbert felt strongly about them becoming
one hospital. He had a way of mediating things and talking to people on
both sides of an issue. The question for him was, what was appropriate; he
advocated for a secular hospital. Arnold described it as "what [Robbert]
was for, rather than what he was against." Robbert thought that there was
an option to raise independent funds. The issue was not without some
controversy and the board resigned after much public upset and invited a
public supervisor to come in and run the hospital in November 2007.

Robbert was an Honorary Life Member of the Huronia Hospitals
Foundation. In appreciation for those running the Foundation, in 1999
Robbert wrote, "As you know the Huronia Hospitals Foundation is
important to me, and I am glad it is in good hands." At the annual meeting,

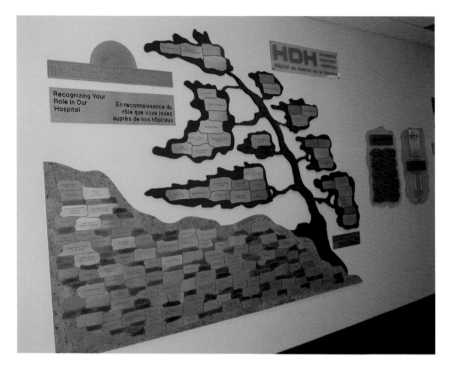

The donor wall at the Huronia District Hospital.

Robbert liked to put the hospital CEOs on the spot to ensure that the hospital was doing everything it needed to do to keep the Foundation running efficiently. He would always say that capital needs, such as basic repairs, were essential to keep the hospital functional, but at every meeting, he emphasized the hospital's responsibility for the best patient care and best equipment. For his commitment and guidance, both Gord Key, retired CEO of Huronia District Hospital, and Dories Shirriff acknowledged that "our hospitals and many others thank God for [Robbert's] presence among us." Robbert replied: "As you know I remain very interested in the health of our hospitals — and the ever-changing scene. The Alliance and its Foundation are good stepping stones, and with vision developed by all concerned, there is no limit to what can be done."

Community Living Huronia

In the early 1960s people with disabilities were not integrated into the school system and they did not mix with other students or learn social skills. In 1961 Community Living Huronia was established to facilitate acceptance, inclusion and support of individuals with exceptionalities as valued citizens. The goal of the organization was "To ensure that people with exceptionalities can live in a state of dignity, with opportunities to participate as effectively as possible in all community activities." According

The Community Living Huronia building on King Street in Midland.

to its mission statement, Community Living Huronia "strives to ensure the availability of supports and services which address the needs of the individuals and their families." The organization is non-profit and supports people from two years of age and older. By 2009 there were 287 adults, and 125 children served by Community Living Huronia, with 19 group homes around the region.

In 1978 Community Living Huronia opened a building on William Street in Midland. Kindred Industries Ltd. (KIL) donated sinks and contributed materials and its staff was involved in raising funds. Robbert oversaw these donations and made connections with KIL and Community Living Huronia. Joyce Hamelin, former executive director of the program, said KIL provided employment opportunities (work programs) to help people with exceptionalities learn how to follow rules, how to be workers, and how to work on an assembly line. According to Tony Vipond, executive director of Community Living Huronia, Robbert recognized that some people would not want to work with handicapped people, so he supported people who did.

Robbert's records indicate that he donated to the organization from 1998 onwards and over the years his donations became an annual contribution. He never specified where the money was to be used. Tony remembered a quiet, generous Robbert who did not say much, but he also recalled a different Robbert who became impassioned when he was working for a cause. He inspired people to do something at the grassroots level to make a difference.

When asked why Robbert valued Community Living Huronia, Joyce said quite simply, "I think he had a tremendous sense of community. I think he had a tremendous sense that everybody should be part of your community and that everybody has a right to that. I think he really understood that … I think it was probably his vision of a community serving everyone and including everyone."

La Maison Rosewood Shelter

La Maison Rosewood Shelter was established in 1985, as an emergency shelter for abused women and their children. The shelter, on Hugel Avenue in Midland, provides 24-hour telephone crisis support, individual counselling, support groups, advocacy on behalf of women and their children, information and referrals, legal support, help with housing and job searches, and public education to increase the awareness of violence against women. Robbert was involved in a hands-off kind of way with the organization since 1997. He was a donor, but he was not actively involved with the organization.

Kathy Willis, executive director of Rosewood, recalled Robbert's involvement in the late 1990s, when she did a direct mail campaign and Robbert donated to that campaign. In the following year, Rosewood had another direct mail campaign, and this time anyone who donated to them in the previous campaign was asked for a 25 per cent increase to the donation. "I had little experience in fundraising at that time and I was much more focused in the service delivery aspects of the organization," she noted. She sent off the letter to Robbert, and he responded with a letter stating that he did not appreciate that Rosewood was so bold and direct as to ask for an increase in funding. Kathy wrote him back with an honest response indicating that they did not have a lot of resources in their organization and they were not trained in philanthropy and fundraising. They were sorry if they had offended him, but this was considered to be the best practice in the fundraising literature. Robbert responded with a cheque with the 25 per cent increase. "For me that was just a really neat thing and I think it spoke to Robbert," Kathy said. "If you could provide him with the logic and the rationale for what you were doing and why you were doing it. He expected accountability and responsibility, but not to a degree that maybe more than he himself would exercise."

Robbert provided annual monetary support. His donations enabled Rosewood to work towards its goal "to end all violence against all women." Although Kathy did not know Robbert on a personal level, "I had a huge amount of respect for the level of contribution he made to this community and how quietly he did that."

Wendat Community Psychiatric Support Programs

Around the mental health facilities in Ontario, there are community programs and resources for people when they move from in-patient to out-patient situations. Often mentally ill people would be in a facility for a number of years, so quite regularly they would move into the community where the hospital was located. Penetanguishene did not develop these services and this caused a continued problem with out-patient services, causing many patients to return to the hospital. In 1989, a group of social workers at the Penetanguishene Mental Health Centre (the largest psychiatric health facility in Ontario) came up with the idea to develop community resources to provide services to assist adults disabled by mental illness so that they could be satisfied and successful where they live, work and socialize.

According to executive director Lorna Tomlinson, "Wendat was, in the very beginning, a service for people with serious mental illness that had been in the mental health centre for quite some time and were now ready for discharge to the community." She said, "As we recognized different needs in the community and different funding opportunities would come along, then we would build our services." Wendat offers a social centre available to out-patients where they provide 24-hour service, and they have individuals on call for crisis intervention. Lorna said 25 per cent of crisis individuals are admitted to the hospital after a psychiatric evaluation and 75 per cent become Wendat clients. The organization also has a psychogeriatric service and works with families with significant mental health issues to support families and to improve access to services required to support these individuals and continue to offer home-based care. Transition service is the other half of what Wendat does. Lorna explained that there is a backlog of senior citizens waiting in hospitals for long-term care, which causes a problem with in-patient care and medical bed use. This has repercussions throughout the health care system.

Lorna first met Robbert in April of 2001 during a capital campaign to expand the Wendat building, as the services outgrew the facilities. "Robbert likes to check you out ... He likes to know who he's giving his money to ... He

The Wendat office on Second Street in Midland.

checks out other people's impression of you and everything, too. He was always very thorough about finding out about a place before he would donate any money. He discriminated a lot. He might give you $10 or he might give you $10,000. It depends on what he thought. He always wanted to see all of your financial statements and everything. He was always very contentious that way in his giving; he wouldn't just blindly give money to anybody." She said, "I'm sure I wrote him a few times and wasn't getting anywhere." During the capital campaign, Robbert's name came up on a list of big donors. Robbert's former Scout and fellow philanthropist Jim Worts suggested to Lorna that she speak Robbert, as she was advised that she would not only need his financial contribution, but also his advice.

The first meeting with Robbert went well. He was encouraging and instructed Lorna to do a feasibility study. "He was always very positive about feasibility studies ... 'You can't proceed without a feasibility study.'" The study provided good leads and solidified a case for support of the building extension. After the meeting he sent one of his infamous letters on Robbert Hartog letterhead, with two or three sentences that were polite and to the point and accompanied with a cheque.

Lorna continued to meet with Robbert every eight or nine months to update him on the progress of the campaign and to seek advice. She said, "He was a great one for suggestions, but boy, you better do his suggestions or ... the next cheque wasn't going to be coming!" Wendat was halfway through the campaign and they seemed to be at the bottom of their funding pool. Lorna said to Robbert, "I've knocked on every door." He replied, "Well then you have to go back."

"Go back where?" Lorna asked.

"Go back to the people's doors you've already knocked on."

"And ask them for more?"

Robbert replied, "Yes! Lorna, Lorna, Lorna. If they gave you money the first time, they gave you money because they thought it was a good idea and a good investment. They'll give you more."

Lorna went back to the office and two days later a letter arrived from Robbert, saying, "You don't have to send someone back to me, here is my cheque." This was a learning experience for Lorna — the theory of going back to donors for additional funds. "He was very encouraging and he was always very instrumental. He gave you really good, concrete suggestions about 'Have you tried this' or 'This is where you need to go' or 'This is what you need to do next.' He was very, very good at being a mentor, at being a teacher." She found out after the campaign that Robbert was checking on the building's progress, driving past the site, contacting individuals that he had encouraged Lorna to get in touch with. It was clear he had his ear to the ground and made sure things were moving along as planned. "You couldn't pull the wool over his eyes, that's for sure!" Lorna exclaimed.

Lorna provided information on Wendat to Robbert early in 2007 and he replied with a letter saying that it was his intention to provide an annual donation (strictly anonymous, of course) to Wendat and leave it to Lorna to decide how to spend it. He said, "Wendat is providing an outstanding service to its clients and it is a distinct pleasure to be able to contribute to it." A month later, Lorna received a cheque with a short note that said "You run an amazingly good organization."

Shelter Now

Shelter Now (formally known as North Simcoe Emergency/Transitional Residential Projects Inc.) was Robbert's last philanthropic project. The organization is a registered charity and a pioneer in the development of supportive housing to end homelessness. Its mission reflects a long-term strategy: "To contribute to a healthy, vibrant community by ensuring those most vulnerable have access to safe, affordable housing and supports." According to Shelter Now's 2008 annual report, "Transitional housing is designed to offer low-cost temporary accommodation for homeless or at-risk individuals and/or families that is combined with case-managed support services, aimed at helping these individuals to transition to long-term permanent housing, self-sufficiency and independence."

The Shelter Now facility, later named Hartog House.

In 2006 Sharon Lapham and Susan MacDonald, both on the board of executives for Shelter Now, set up a meeting with Robbert to propose the idea of building a 10 to 12-unit affordable transitional housing facility. They went to Robbert's house in Perkinsfield and presented the information to him. He read it all over, handed the papers back, sat back in his chair and said, "Do you really think this meets the need?" He kept bringing up "the need" and Sharon was not sure what he was getting at with this statement. Finally, he sat back and said, "I'm not sure if I've made myself clear. I'm prepared to fund this 100 per cent. I just want to know that you're building it to meet the long term needs. Is this enough?" Sharon Lapham was from a social service perspective where "you never have enough," so she was shocked by Robbert's reaction. She said, "His thinking was, you never build a factory without thinking for the long term. He said, 'So I'm not going to have my name attached unless you're planning for the long-term." Sharon Lapham and Susan MacDonald went back to the board and decided they could easily double the capacity and easily fill it.

The board of executives took Robbert's advice and the transitional apartment complex has 20 units. The building includes office space that is rented out to local services, such as the mental health support unit, and case management services, which helps offset the rent of the units and provides sustainability and services for the community. The apartments are linked to such services for the tenants to maintain their housing, restore their health, and regain their economic independence — all of which are vital to help people overcome homelessness.

After re-evaluating the scope of the project, the board members of Shelter Now met with Robbert and with Reinhart Weber (Robbert's friend and fellow philanthropist) in 2007. The two decided they would split the costs 50/50 between them. Sharon said, "They were both really keen about the project. They said, 'We're prepared to fund the capital costs of the building.'" Robbert wrote in a letter dated June 20, 2007, "This is an impressive project that deserves support (and as Mr. Weber indicated that both the Weber Foundation and I are willing to support such a well-thought-out and properly organized project) with serious contributions … The Weber Foundation and I are very interested in ascertaining that the right leadership exists — the finances will follow, believe us."

Robbert and Reinhart were decisive in their support, once their concerns and questions had been addressed. Susan said, "[Robbert] had no patience for going around in circles on items. He would say, 'This is what we want to do. Let's do it' … There was another side of him that was very quietly supportive and he never forgot you, he always stayed in touch. That is such a lovely characteristic." After Robbert and Reinhart's contributions were secured, Shelter Now had almost all of the funding for the project. Robbert was a task force member for the Shelter Now Feasibility Study in May 2007, but this was a rare case in fundraising where an organization launched a feasibility study, but did not proceed because it got all of its money in two donations. "This was extremely impressive that this project, and it's a huge project, has been done almost entirely with private dollars," Sharon said.

Robbert's involvement with community housing needs started with a small involvement with Community Link, a multi-service organization that provides programs, support and resources that promote self-sufficiency and seeks to significantly improve the quality of life for members of North Simcoe. Homelessness is a serious problem in the Midland area. In 2006, some 2,000 individuals were looking for housing through Community Link. Sharon said, "This area has a larger-than-average percentage of people with disabilities. Many of those people have a mental illness, because of the proximity to the mental health hospital … There is also lower-than-average income levels." A substantial number of people struggle from month to month to make ends meet, with 30 per cent or more of their income going towards paying rent.

Shelter Now was proposed late 2006, and the campaign did not last long. By 2008 they were breaking ground at 850 Hartman Drive in Midland. Shelter Now is already looking beyond the initial project to develop other marketable, affordable, supported housing projects. This apartment complex is considered phase one, which is aimed to address long-term community needs. For phase two and three, Shelter Now plans to develop family complexes and then single residential occupancy with permanent units and support. Their focus is on a whole range of services. According to Sharon, "[Phase one] is seen as just one piece of a range of options that you need to have available in a community."

Robbert had a strong understanding of the needs of his community and he thought about the big picture. He valued the strong leadership of the executive board members of Shelter Now and he believed in the long-term success of the project. Susan said, "Robbert has a very good sense of all the pieces that are needed to make a healthy community… He had a special understanding for hard-to-serve populations and I think the big point would be that he knows its not as easy to fundraise for those, so he's willing to put some support behind that." Shelter Now is a local solution to a local problem that Robbert believed in.

St. Paul's United Church

Robbert's business and philanthropic commitments often required him to travel extensively. However, every Sunday that he was home, he loyally attended St. Paul's United Church. Before moving to Midland, Robbert was a member of Rosedale United Church, but in September 1962, he wrote Reverend Morden in Midland, saying, "Now that I am settled in Midland I would very much like to join St. Paul's United Church as soon as convenient." During his time at St. Paul's he was a member of the Trustees Committee, and chairman of the board for a time; he was head of the Finance Committee, a member of the Official Board, and a member of the Christian Education Committee. In May 1963, he signed up to be an usher; he noted that he would be away several months of the year, but he would do what he could when he was available. When he ran meetings at the church, they were in true Robbert fashion — short and efficient. He was diligent in sending his apologies whenever he would be out of town for a meeting. His records indicate that in 1997 he

Robbert's church, St. Paul's United Church in downtown Midland.

began donating to St. Paul's on an annual basis. He would make quarterly contributions, which were normally divided between the Mission and Service Fund (which supports the mission work of the United Church, and the organization of the United Church, education of ministry, mission congregations in Canada and outreach projects) and general purposes. Sometimes he would make a special contribution to relieve the church of a deficit it had incurred. His conditions were that such donations remain completely anonymous and that the relief be referred to as general support from the congregation, not from an individual. Robbert said, "I hate deficits, and as long as I can, I will do my utmost to kill them."

When Robbert left Midland for Cambridge in the 1970s, he continued to donate to St. Paul's as an adherent. When he arrived in Cambridge he joined the First United Church, on Wellington Street, where he made generous weekly contributions and donated to summer projects. In a letter to the treasurer on June 1, 1978, Robbert said, "As the summer months are always difficult for a church treasurer, I wish to prepay some of my weekly offerings and hereby enclose a cheque for 20 weeks — as usual, two-thirds is for local use, and one-third for M & M [Ministry and Mission]."

When he returned to Midland in the 1980s, he again became involved with St. Paul's. At that time St. Paul's was looking into hiring a second minister. Reverend Cliff Pendlebury was considering joining the ministry at St. Paul's if there was financial support for him to do so. His first encounter with Robbert was during a meeting in the church lounge, discussing this issue. He said, "I am sitting there and thinking 'This isn't going too well because it all points to how's this money going to come in through the membership of the congregation.' Then there's a gentleman sitting at the back of the room, and I didn't know who he was … This man got up and he said, 'I think that we have to act in faith and believe that if we start this ministry that the money will come in to support the ministry'" Not realizing that Robbert was the person that he was and so influential in the community, Cliff thought that this is the kind of person needed in the church. Shortly after this meeting, he applied for the position and became a minister at St. Paul's.

On Pentecost Sunday, members of the congregation read the Pentecostal story in several different languages. Cliff asked Robbert one year to participate and read a passage in Dutch. He agreed, saying, "I'll do it in Dutch, but actually my Bible was the French Bible." Robbert had become a Christian during the Second World War, presumably during his time in Paris, but he never spoke of his conversion. Cliff presumed that Robbert made a profession of faith in Europe during the war or when he came to Toronto and joined the Rosedale United Church. Cliff and Robbert never got into deep discussions of faith. Many of Robbert's relatives were Jewish, but he did not discuss faith. They spoke about what they had in common, rather than their differences.

Cliff speculated on why Robbert may have been attracted to the United Church when he came from Europe. "I think what might have appealed to him was more or less the freedom of the United Church," he said. "The United Church is probably the most liberal church in Canada; it is a wide and diverse church as well and it is the largest Protestant denomination in Canada. Also, I think because the United Church had a strong sense for social justice. I think that's what really helped Robbert. It was a hands-on kind of thing. Projects like Canadian Crossroads International." Robbert had this mindset of "How do we help out?" which is a strong value of the church.

Robbert was an active participant in the church, but he was also a private man whom no one really got to know. He often sat in the same pew and came and left church quietly. "The most remarkable trait of his character was his humility, his constant desire and effort to stay below the radar and do his good works in his own quiet, effective manner, without telling anybody about it, or having anybody notice, if he could," remarked Tom Hazell (a friend and fellow parishioner). "He was a great supporter and huge benefactor of the church. He was a very loyal attendee and gave great direction." Robbert would attend church when he was in town, but Cliff remembers often shaking hands with Robbert at the end of a service and Robbert remarking that he was off to Thailand, or Egypt, on CESO business. His travels made him wise to social issues around the world. Early on in his ministry Cliff gave a sermon at a gathering on social justice. He talked about the inequalities in the world and the basic differences between the rich and the poor. After the service, Robbert came out and shook Cliff's hand and said, "Actually, it's a little bit worse than what you said."

To take action against social injustice, Robbert enjoyed a hands-on approach. In May 2006, the Government of Canada requested support from churches across the country with the resettlement of Karen refugees (the Karen are an ethnic group in Burma and Thailand). A long-standing conflict between the Burmese military regime, which has held power since 1962, and the Karen National Union is considered one of the world's longest-running civil wars. There are numerous reports of ethnic cleansing and hundreds of thousands of Burmese and ethnic refugees have flooded to western Thailand. Members of St. Paul's congregation wanted to help, and the Outreach Committee began working with the United Church Refugee Office and Citizenship and Immigration Canada to support this plan. Ken and Jane Woods worked internationally in Thailand, India and the Philippines, among other nations, with various international organizations, providing outreach to the less fortunate. Jane was in a refugee camp in Thailand in the early 1990s, when she met a woman named Lah Eh Shee. Years later, Ken and Jane were able to find this woman and the church worked to sponsor her and her husband, Kaw Khee Lar, and their two young children, Paw Roe Shee and Kaw Lah Shee. Successful applications to sponsor refugees were far more likely to come from large urban centres, so the committee was worried that they would not receive government funding for the sponsorship in Midland.

Ken wanted to speak with Robbert about the project. He knew Robbert through their involvement with Canadian Crossroads International in the 1960s. Ken went to his house and explained the situation and within 15 minutes Robbert said, "Of course, don't worry about it."

Top: Kaw Khee Lar (left), Lah Eh Shee (right) and their children (centre) Paw Roe Shee and Kaw Lah Shee

Below: Robbert (far left) at dinner with the newly arrived refugee family.

"Well, Robbert, I have to worry about it because when you don't have the money, you have to worry about it."

"Ken, don't worry about it. Well, what might it cost to support a family?"

Ken gave him an estimate and Robbert again replied, "Don't worry about it."

With that, Ken was able to go back and make a presentation to the church board and assure the board members that the project would be funded.

After many talks with the government agency, St. Paul's was denied funding for the sponsorship because Midland was viewed as an undesirable city to support the refugees. Members of the St. Paul's Refugee Committee, including Robbert, then launched a private sponsorship, funded through the United Church of Canada, and the congregation of St. Paul's, with Robbert being a major financial contributor. The committee met once a month. Within a year, the family arrived in Midland, in June 2007. According to Jane and Ken, the important thing to Robbert was that the family have a great experience in Midland and that they were properly introduced to their new surroundings. They had to understand living in a house with electricity and refrigeration. They lived on fish paste in the camp, so it was quite a transition. In a letter to Ken, Robbert said, "I am looking forward to welcoming a family here, where there is a future and welcoming enthusiasm."

Robbert's role on the committee was to assist with job placement in Midland for the parents of the refugee family. Lah Eh Shee worked cleaning houses, but she started to become interested in further education. She was a schoolteacher in Thailand and she was interested in employment in education, child care, or working with seniors. In January 2007, Robbert expressed his desire for a scholarship to be made for Lah Eh Shee. Kaw Khee Lar worked at a local marina and then he was offered a job at a factory in Penetanguishene. The children both adjusted well to their new

Lah Eh Shee (left), Kaw Khee Lar (right), and their children (centre) Paw Roe Shee and Kaw Lah Shee at Nathan Phillips Square in Toronto.

surroundings, and the family received English as a Second Language support. In a letter to Ken in September 2007, Robbert wrote, "The progress from a camp environment to a free citizenship, living in Midland is fantastic — and with a bit of effort by us all it is looking like (thanks to a large extent to Jane and you) a true success story."

Robbert and the Liberal Party

In the late 1960s and early 1970s, Robbert was an active member of the Liberal Party and he donated to the Ontario Liberals. Although he held Liberal beliefs throughout his life, his formal involvement with the party ended in the late 1970s. He was elected president of Simcoe East Riding Liberal Association at an annual meeting in March 1966 and he was elected president of the Simcoe North Federal Liberal Association at the annual meeting in Orillia in April 1971. He was president of the Liberal Party in Simcoe North for two terms in the late 1960s and early 1970s. Robbert attended the 1968 Liberal leadership convention and initially supported Mitchell Sharp, but when Sharp dropped out of the race, Robbert backed Pierre Elliott Trudeau. Early in the week of the convention, Gil Robillard and Robbert were in the elevator going to the 21st floor, when a young man, in his early 30s, entered the elevator. Gil, with a friendly approach, said to him, "I know you, I am Gil Robillard, the mayor of Penetanguishene" — but the man did not respond until just before the elevator stopped at the 14th floor, and he left the elevator, saying, "I am your tax inspector" (and the door closed). Gil's face got a bit pale — and when they left the elevator he asked Robbert if he thought the young man was a tax inspector. Robbert laughed and said, "In a way he is. He is the Minister of Revenue; his name is Jean Chrétien." The two saw quite a bit more of this young man, as they all worked for Mitchell Sharp and helped get Trudeau elected.

According to Francis St. Amant, an active Liberal Party member in Simcoe North, Robbert engaged with Trudeau and supported him throughout his leadership. John Gammell, also a Liberal Party member in the North Simcoe area, believed that Robbert's leadership in the party attracted non-Liberals, who converted because of Trudeau and because of the mobilization of a stronger campaign organization around Robbert and the industries in Midland. Like his draw to the United Church, Robbert agreed with the Liberal Party's emphasis on helping people, not necessarily socialism, but helping people help themselves.

Other Involvements

The list of Robbert's involvements is long and varied. In the 1960s he was instrumental in providing credibility and funding for the Penetanguishene Industrial Park. He sat on the planning committee for excavations on Heritage Christian Island as part of a University of Western Ontario archeological survey. He was a member and donor of the Huronia Museum in Midland. In 1990 he made an anonymous donation to upgrade the washrooms at the facility. In 1985 he was on the board of directors as the representative from Tiny Township for the Local Employment Assistance and Development program.

He played both large and small roles in various charities in his community and throughout the country. For example, he was a loyal supporter of the committee "Netherlands Bazaar," held each year in Thornhill, Ontario. In a letter to the president of the committee in 1997, Robbert wrote, "I still recall the first announcement 39 years ago, when I worked at Kitchen Installations Ltd. It is a pleasure to enclose a cheque to assist this most worthwhile endeavour."

Robbert could not and did not support every charitable organization that solicited his help. He acknowledged that the were many worthy causes that needed help, but he made decisions based on his vision of his community or country and where he wanted to focus his efforts. He required background information on the organization, as he liked to educate himself on where his money would be used. Robbert wrote to an organization he decided not to fund in 1999, saying, "As you may realize I have had to rationalize my charitable givings, and decided on a few organizations, rather than spreading my givings too wide. [Your organization] is not amongst the associations I support, but that is certainly not a reflection on the merit of your association. However, it is, unfortunately, necessary to eliminate from my list certain most worthwhile organizations, like yours." He respected well-led organizations and campaigns and those causes often garnered his support.

John Lister, director and manager of the Georgian College capital campaign, is a seasoned fundraiser who worked with Robbert on several projects, including the YMCA and the Wye Marsh. "Robbert is my icon, my model; it doesn't get any better than him," said John. Robbert taught him many lessons about fundraising, especially how to accept and respect a gift. John said that Robbert believed that in order to raise money, it was not about games or tactics, but it is about sincerity and integrity. In order to keep Robbert interested, a charity needed to do its homework and listen carefully to his words. He needed to trust the organization he was giving to; therefore, leadership was everything to him. He needed to see that an organization could make a project work within time constraints and a budget.

Robbert was interested in making the whole community better for the people he cared about, and the people who worked for him. He saw what the community needed, whether it was improved hospital facilities, a well-maintained United Church, or support for individuals involved with Community Living Huronia, Wendat, Shelter Now, or Rosewood. By lending his name to many projects in the community, he added credibility to capital campaigns and fundraisers. Robbert's wide-range community involvement helped the North Simcoe area to be a healthy, active, viable, and caring community. His involvement in charities in Midland showed his commitment to the community and reached many causes and people of all ages. He quietly used his involvement to inspire others to give back to the community in which they live.

CHAPTER NINE

Global Citizen

R obbert Hartog supported local organizations to sustain a thriving community, but he also reached out nationally and internationally. Robbert saw the big picture. He wanted a whole community, as well as a united world. His international travels exposed him to the harsh realities of poverty, violence, and injustice, which strengthened his resolve to take action. Robbert helped because there was a need and he saw that need. Through his work with Canadian Crossroads International (CCI), Frontiers Foundation, and the Canadian Executive Service Organization (CESO), Robbert embodied global citizenship. His duty and privilege was to share and grow with others around the world.

Canadian Crossroads International

In 1958 a group of men, including Robbert, gathered at a United Church in Toronto to listen to the American civil rights activist and Operation Crossroads Africa founder, Dr. James Robinson. An African-American Baptist minister, Dr. Robinson believed that North Americans needed to work alongside Africans to build infrastructure. He also sought to bring black and white youths together during a time of social unrest in North

Robbert listening closely to a client on a Canadian Executive Service Organization trip.

America. The goal was to send people to Africa as peers to learn and to share their experiences with others. That night, the men raised $5,000 and Dr. Robinson asked them to use that money to form the Canadian chapter. In 1958, Peter Paris, from Nova Scotia, was the first Canadian to go to Africa as part of the new chapter. Robbert became the founding chair of the board in 1959. In November 1962, as the guest speaker at the Midland Y's Men's Club, Robbert discussed interracial relations and especially the role of Canadians in "Crossroads of Africa," a commitment that Robbert would work to fulfill.

In 1969, Operations Crossroads Africa changed to a separate status and the chapter became Canadian Crossroads International. CCI reaches out to organizations and people throughout the developing world, including placements for over 2,700 volunteers. Since 1967, volunteers have completed over 80,000 assignments in some 50 countries. The statistics are staggering and the need for such an organization is great: 38 million people are infected with HIV worldwide; more than half of the world's population live on less than $2 U.S. a day; one child dies every 3 seconds as a result of extreme poverty; millions of people do not enjoy basic human rights. Robbert was attracted to CCI as part of a global response to promote human rights, eliminate poverty, and reduce the impact of HIV/AIDS. Using a partnership model, which always appealed to Robbert, CCI invests its resources to strengthen women's rights, mitigate the impact of HIV/AIDS and reduce poverty, particularly in West Africa, Southern Africa and the Andean region of South America. Central to the partnership is the exchange of skilled volunteers and staff. With CCI's support, partners in developing countries select Canadian partner organizations across the country that are working on similar issues to help develop programs and goals. Each year, CCI brings partners from developing countries to Canada to work with Canadian partners; meanwhile, Canadians are sent to African and South America countries to work with local organizations. Placements can vary from several weeks to a year, depending on the project. The foundation of CCI is the partnerships that build a global network of people and organizations working together to address international issues.

Robbert was on CCI's Advisory Committee and in 2004 he was on the board for the Leadership Gift Committee. According to the former national director of CCI, Lisa Boyle, "He was extraordinarily valuable to the committee and CCI." As he was involved with CCI since its inception, he recognized the overall importance of giving to the organization. Robbert wanted CCI to be ambitious and he believed in the organization's

objectives. On their first meeting, Robbert said to Karen Takacs (executive director of CCI), "You know what, Karen. You have to remain relevant
and that's what you are doing. Don't worry, be bold, don't be afraid to ask."
From this first impression, Karen quickly recognized Robbert as a kind,
caring and determined man. He encouraged others to give to CCI, and
he led by example, donating his money and his time for various meetings.
Karen explained that he also pledged the largest gift the organization has ever
received. Robbert did not want recognition and he told Karen that it was up
to the board how to allocate the money. He said, "This is really for the board
to decide. I believe that Canadians need to see themselves as global citizens,
in particular in this day and age, and that is what I want to support. It is up
to you how to spend the money…That is what I am investing in."

Karen said that Robbert did not have a particular focus on any one
issue that CCI addressed, although micro-credit loan programs in Bolivia
and West Africa especially interested him. He left the direction of his funds
to the board, but not because he was uninterested. "He was a smart man,"
Karen said. "It wasn't like he was naïve or didn't care. He did and he asked
tough questions. He was no fool, that's for sure. So, to have his vote of
confidence meant a considerable amount to us, especially because he had
been involved since the beginning. It also just speaks to his generosity as a
philanthropist. There aren't many like him." Lisa emphasized the importance

A group of Canadian Crossroads
International supporters.

of following Robbert's "crisp advice." She said, "We all felt very honoured when he would come to a meeting or event. We felt compelled to follow up on any suggestions that he had … There was no doubting that what he suggested you should follow through on because it would be fruitful." Robbert travelled from Midland to Toronto for CCI meetings. He would travel early in the morning, through snowstorms, to be punctual for an 8 a.m. meeting. Robbert strongly believed in CCI and it was apparent in his active involvement with the organization. He never went to Africa on a CCI mission, but he supported the organization to allow it to expand and continue to strive to reach its objectives.

To Karen, Robbert epitomized what it meant to be a global citizen. He lived it through his humility, generosity, and keen interest in the world. He fundamentally believed that all Canadians needed to be global citizens and he wanted to ensure that CCI continued its good work.

Frontiers Foundation (Operation Beaver)

Charles Catto, founding director of Frontiers Foundation, was familiar with CCI and had attended a meeting in the mid-1960s. He understood the value of partnerships in Africa, but he wondered, too, how people could similarly help their own struggling communities in Canada and aboriginal communities in other countries. In 1964, Charles founded Frontiers Foundation and began work on "Operation Beaver," a non-profit aboriginal voluntary service that promotes the advancement of economically and socially disadvantaged communities. As it was explained in 1969, "Through the Operation Beaver program, with volunteers from across the globe, [Frontiers Foundation] work[s] with aboriginal communities to provide affordable housing and improvements in education. With the support of government and charitable donations, both from the private sector and individuals, volunteers operate within Canadian borders, and overseas in tangible advancement projects in impoverished communities." There is a partnership between host communities on community-based development projects, such as building and/or renovating homes, or organizing activities for local youth. Volunteers and members of the host communities come together and build homes and exchange and share cross-cultural experiences.

Robbert was drawn to the organization in the 1960s because he was interested in the Third World in Canada. He and Charles Catto had the kind of relationship where if Frontiers Foundation was in need, Robbert would be a phone call away to help Charles. Robbert did not waste words when they spoke; he would get right to the point and say, "What is your immediate need?" In a letter to Robbert in September 1998, Charles lamented, "There are times when we do not know how we shall survive. But we never doubted that we are doing Christ's work in this wonderful country. As much as anyone in Canada, you have maintained our faith and hope." Charles kept Robbert up to date on what was happening with the organization and Robbert would reply to his letters with a donation. In October

The Dodge Pickup truck donated by Robbert to Frontiers Foundation.

2004 Robbert wrote to Charles, saying, "I leave it entirely in your hands how to allocate the proceeds. As always it is a pleasure to be able to assist you in your outstanding endeavours." Since his funds were never allocated, Charles felt that the organization could give Robbert credit for almost anything Frontiers Foundation has accomplished in the past 45 years. Over the years he not only made financial contributions, but donated a Dodge minivan and a four-wheel drive diesel Dodge pickup to aid volunteers in their work in remote communities.

Robbert often made Charles feel like he was the only person in the world, because it seemed like he was always thinking of him. Robbert had this effect on many people, as he was never too busy for people and organizations he valued in his life. He was also instrumental in securing funding from Fairfax Financial for a Toronto housing project in 2000. Fairfax matched Robbert's donation to the project. For a time Robbert was a member of the Fairfax Donations Committee and he encouraged the committee to contribute to a few of the organizations he supported.

Robbert was an informal advisor to Charles though he did not have any official role in the organization. However, both Charles and Frontiers Foundation executive director Marco Guzman felt a connection with Robbert. Marco passionately described his first meeting with Robbert: "When I met him, right away he shook hands with me and the friendship, you can feel it." Robbert believed in "doing" rather than "talking" and he respected Frontiers Foundation for its action-based objectives to better serve Canadian and international communities.

Canadian Executive Service Organization

When scheduling meetings with friends and associates, Robbert would often comment on his availability, saying he would be out of the country to Colombia or Egypt or Thailand for several weeks. Of course, he would rarely elaborate on his business there, aside from mentioning that it was as a volunteer for Canadian Executive Service Organization (CESO). CESO is a volunteer-based not-for profit organization founded in 1967. Volunteer Advisers (VAs), mainly retired men and women from Canada, offer their expertise to businesses, governments and other organizations in developing nations, new free-market economies, and to Canadian aboriginal communities and businesses. VAs serve as short-term consultants from three weeks to three months with a client. CESO's overall vision is for its VAs to help local businesses and governments, to thereby enhance development of economic and social conditions in developing countries. From 1985 to 2006 Robbert undertook 13 assignments as a VA in eight different countries. His role was to help these businesses grow and to problem solve using his expertise in stainless steel product production. Robbert described CESO as "a volunteer-based organization with a mission to transfer Canadian expertise to businesses, communities and organizations in order to help them achieve their goals of economic self-sufficiency."

There are over 2,700 volunteers from coast to coast currently on the CESO roster. The organization uses from 500 to 600 volunteers per year to deliver its programs. In early 1985 Robbert was put on a roster of volunteers and remained on its roster for 21 years, in which time CESO completed 22,000 missions. When the organization gave him an assignment, he was responsible for diligently and honestly applying his skills and expertise to help the client who requested an advisor. CESO briefed clients before a VA arrived, emphasizing that the assigned VA was a specially qualified person who was eager to help by sharing experience and skills on a voluntary basis. CESO normally paid for the airfare of the VA, and the client was responsible for providing appropriate lodging, as well as meal arrangements. In return the VA provided a transfer of knowledge that clients in developing nations could otherwise not afford. Secretary, treasurer, and chief financial officer of CESO, Terry Brackenridge, described the living arrangements of VAs on assignments, saying, "If [Robbert] was over there on a CESO assignment, you are working in the plant with all the people. When he goes over there, the client pays for meals and accommodations so they would house the volunteer, not in a five-star hotel. They might be in an apartment or if the owner of the business has a boarding house. There have been cases where they would be billeted in the owner of the business's own house living with the family. But usually we try to give them clean, safe accommodation." CESO arranges for the volunteers to find suitable projects, as each country has a CESO representative for a client to contact directly. Requests are sent to the head office in Toronto and then recruiters go through the roster for the most qualified volunteer listed. When the assignment is completed, the VA provides a report with recommendations to the client.

On March 4, 1985, Robbert embarked on his first CESO assignment to Colombia to help a company named Rivesa, a kitchen systems manufacturer. That assignment lasted approximately a month. Robbert's VA report from Rivesa read, "Mr. Hartog is a very good volunteer and representative of Canada. His knowledge and experience in the requested field is wonderful, so his assistance to the company was really successful. Our client was very satisfied and grateful for his help and collaboration." Dan Haggerty (president and CEO of CESO from 1985 to 1998) echoed these comments: "He was always a very genuine person. Very caring. He was never defending or selfish. He was just a generous, warm person and a pleasure to work with."

Robbert travelled all over the world with CESO. While away he would keep in touch with his secretary in Midland to keep abreast of any happenings at home, including any invitations to functions and information on local politics and the frigid Midland winter weather. On assignments he provided techniques to improve production process and efficiency. He would usually be sent to address a specific problem. For example, in March 1991, he travelled to Malaysia to help a company called Laid Gas Sales and Service. Robbert was asked to assist with casting electrode plating. After his stay, Robbert wrote the company a note praising their work ethic. "The end of a very pleasant three weeks spent in your (sometimes hot) factory. It is always good to listen to, and experiment with, different ideas."

Robbert often corresponded with clients if he later came across information that would be useful. After an assignment in Egypt with Helco Metals in 1994, Robbert wrote his hosts, "After a long day of travelling, I arrived home and I wanted to thank you most sincerely for your friendly reception and great co-operation. I am trying to find the latest books on deep drawing, which I will send to you. The experience in Egypt was

Robbert with the clients he assisted on a CESO trip in Colombia.

Robbert during his trip as a VA to Uruguay.

most interesting and I will always recall the friendship of many people. If I can be of any assistance to you in the future, please let me know." In a correspondence with Rodolfo P. Benas S. A., a company Robbert was a VA with in 1991 in Uruguay, Robbert referred to his "Benas friends." While in Malaysia Robbert wrote Rodolfo, saying, "I have decided that I prefer Angela's coffee and Salus mineral water over cold Chinese tea!!"

Along with being a committed VA, Robbert was also a member of the board of directors of CESO from the late 1980s to the early 1990s. He chaired the board from 1991 to 1993. "Things ran very smoothly when he was around. While he was chair of the board there were never any conflicts with anyone," said Terry. He continued,

> I really liked the man. To me he was one of our better board chairs because he was knowledgeable of CESO. He had been there. He had come through the ranks as a volunteer first. We have had some other board chairs that have come right into the organization on the board because they are vice-president or president of some other organization that we would like to be associated with. But, they don't understand volunteerism the way Robbert did. They don't understand what the volunteer gives up or how much they share their knowledge with other people. Robbert believed in CESO and its importance and effectiveness in the world. If you go to the lengths that he did, did the number of assignments that he did as a volunteer, giving up your time and energy and are still willing to sit on the board, you believe. No, he made a difference.

On May 31, 1999, after turning 80, Robbert wrote to CESO, announcing his retirement as a VA. "There is a time for starting a CESO adventure and a time for closing that chapter — and I believe the time has come for me to request that you remove my name from the active roster. It has been a pleasure to participate in a number of projects. My (now more passive) interest in CESO remains high." Between 1985 and 1999, Robbert had completed a dozen assignments in Columbia, Thailand,

Uruguay, Peru, Romania, the Philippines, and Egypt. In 2006 a keen recruiter asked Robbert for some recommended names to assist a stainless steel sink manufacturer named Industrias Guinovart, in Columbia. The names Robbert suggested turned out to be unavailable, so he suggested that he might be available — and so his last assignment became a reality. Before his departure, Robbert wrote, "I am off for five weeks for a work project in South America — perhaps the last one I can do properly?" Having an 87-year-old active VA was unheard of for CESO, and a condition of the trip was that Robbert supply his own health coverage. Medical coverage out of province was quite expensive, totalling almost $3,000, a cost Robbert was willing to absorb for the project. In March 2006 he travelled to Columbia to advise Industrias Guinovart, the small company of about 100 or so employees, and said, "It went quite well — with the normal hitches one encounters in a developing country."

CESO assignments represented a substantial investment in the future of a client organization by the client itself, the VA and the government of Canada. Robbert believed in supporting his own country, as well as people, businesses, and economies all over the world. He thought that Canadians should see themselves as global citizens. He saw it as his duty to help others, regardless of their race, class, creed, economic standing, or geography. He travelled the world and volunteered his time with enthusiasm for a better world.

Client Name	Country	Start Date
Inelso Ltda.	Colombia	11 Apr 86
Inelso Ltda.	Colombia	13 July 86
Socoda Ltda.	Colombia	05 Oct 87
Jaguar Industries	Thailand	02 Oct 89
Rodolfo P Benas S.A.	Uruguay	03 Jan 91
Laid Gas Sales & Service	Malaysia	28 Feb 91
Mireya S.A.	Uruguay	05 Jan 92
Corporation Progreso	Peru	18 Oct 92
Imsat S.A.	Romania	16 Jan 93
Helco Metals	Egypt	03 Oct 94
Ramcar Inc.	Philippines	21 Oct 96
Industrias Guinovart	Colombia	01 Mar 06

CHAPTER TEN

Thailand

At 6:40 a.m. on November 21, 2006, Thai Airways flight 795 from Los Angeles touched down in Bangkok, Thailand. The long trip required a lot of patience, which Robbert self-admittedly lacked. He sat in business class, as it was customary for him to upgrade on flights, particularly those longer than six hours. He would often spend such a trip reading (he enjoyed mystery novels); if, after reading a chapter into a book he did not like it, he would mutter "Idiot!" and shove the book into the seat pocket in front of him for another passenger to find. After flying for over 20 hours from Toronto to Bangkok, Robbert stretched his stiff legs and walked into Suvarnabhumi Airport. The large dome-like ceilings echoed with the bustle of morning travellers. After getting his baggage, Robbert made his way through the large doors into the International Arrivals. He scanned the crowd of people and soon saw a familiar face, which made him smile with delight. At 87 years old, Robbert had made a long journey that is intimidating to seasoned travellers. He had made that trip nearly every year for two decades, so he was not about to let his age stop him from seeing old friends whom he considered family. This chapter provides a detailed, insider's account of Robbert's influence on one important company that allows the reader to catch a glimpse of the wide range of his involvement and his personal commitment to those with whom he worked.

Suchitra, Sornchai, and Robbert touring the temple complex with the guide.

Above: The Thai family greeting Robbert at the airport.

Below: Robbert (left) enjoying an authentic Thai meal.

Scrap metal being recycled at a Jaguar factory.

Robbert's influence was strongly felt and valued at Jaguar Industries in Bangkok, Thailand. After his first trip on a Canadian Executive Service Organization assignment in 1989, Robbert returned to Thailand nearly every year for the next 20 years. If he could not make the trip one year, the client family would come to Canada and visit him. This relationship began with business, but developed into a lasting friendship, as Robbert became an endless source of guidance and support. Indeed, at Jaguar Industries Robbert is considered a family member.

During the first few months of 1989, a fellow Volunteer Advisor (VA) of Robbert's at the CESO told him that while on assignment in Thailand the local CESO representative had asked the VA to accompany her to a prospective client, Jaguar Industries, on the outskirts of Bangkok. It appeared that the company had some problems in deep drawing stainless steel (for pots and food-carriers), as the texture of some products was cracking after production. Knowing that this was Robbert's specialty, the VA suggested that Robbert could assist this client. The VA sent him some pictures and wrote that the enterprises looked like a scrapyard. When Robbert returned from Bangkok in late 1989, he told his colleague that he was right. It was a scrapyard, and behind it was a stainless steel product plant.

Robbert vividly recalled first arriving in Bangkok in October 1989, after many hours of plane travel. Greeting Robbert was a CESO representative, the wife of the Jaguar Industries owner (and company controller), Mrs. Suchitra, as well as the sales manager (who was present because he spoke English). After enjoying coffee together, his hosts took Robbert to a hotel close to the sales office. That afternoon Robbert met the owner, Mr. Sornchai, and they visited the plant. It was the start of a lasting friendship.

Robbert's previous assignments with CESO had been in Spanish-speaking countries, and this was his first experience with a serious linguistic problem. He overcame it with lots of drawings, the use of illustrations from the engineer's study books, and plenty of gestures. Sornchai and Robbert could only understand each other about 30 to 40 per cent of the time, according to Mr. Rittichai (Sornchai's son), so they needed the assistance of a translator whenever possible. Sornchai was eager to learn from Robbert and respected his advice. The Thai people were extremely hospitable and pleasant, and Robbert enjoyed his visits with Sornchai and Suchitra. At their dining table, Robbert usually sat in the same chair, which allowed

Top: Sornchai, Robbert, and Suchitra dining together.

Middle: Robbert, Sornchai, and Suchitra on a day trip in Thailand.

Bottom: Robbert (centre) participating in Thai culture.

him to see the mounted television. During most dinners, the three of them discussed how Jaguar Industries could improve its quality. Suchitra loved vegetables and Robbert joked that vegetables were the food for rabbits. For this, he endearingly called her "rabbit." Robbert got in the habit of checking the back of his utensils for the Jaguar engravings, and during his travels all over the world, he continued this ritual.

Robbert learned that Sornchai wanted to use a large quantity of round blanks from the scrapyard. The blanks had been intended to become hubcaps (which require hard steel) and after many experiments it became obvious that they could use these blanks only for plates. It was a good opportunity for Robbert to explain that quality requires predictable input, which is not always found in scrap material. Sornchai was a self-made man, with strong common sense and an entrepreneurial spirit. He and Robbert hit it off, and after a week Robbert no longer was an outside consultant but had become "Uncle Robbert" — to everyone there.

They made some excellent progress during this first visit and Robbert left Sornchai with a confidential final report listing specific recommendations — which he followed for several years. To solve the deep-drawing problem, Robbert advised Sornchai to use a grid to see where the cracking occurred. Using this technique, the cracking disappeared. The six weeks in Bangkok, thanks to several family outings to Beachos on weekends, passed rapidly. At the end they had a farewell dinner, with gifts and mutual expressions of appreciation.

Robbert, Suchitra, and Akachai together.

Two years later, after a CESO project in Malaysia, Robbert visited Thailand as a tourist — and of course went to the Jaguar plant. It was heartening for him to see the progress, to learn that they were holding Quality Circles, and to view that they had followed through on his recommendations. It was also obvious that the company was enjoying better profits.

Later, after Sornchai and Robbert exchanged many faxes, Robbert received a request to help Jaguar with a specific die problem which was restricting their much-expanded flatware production. Things were going well at Jaguar and the cost of providing air tickets was no longer a problem for the family, although Robbert insisted on paying his own way. He went to Thailand again, this time not as a CESO consultant, but as a friend and advisor. He stayed with the family, who now lived close to the plant and had a room for him in an adjoining prefab. The solution to the die problem was easy once Sornchai and Robbert talked through the problem; use a "tough" die material, not a "very hard" one. After establishing a relationship with an internationally well-known tool steel corporation, the right material solved the problem.

The next encounter came when Robbert's Jaguar family visited North America as tourists, and spent three days in the Toronto area, where he joined them. He now referred to Sornchai, Suchitra, their two sons, Mr. Akachai and Mr. Rittichai, and their daughter, Ms. Rasamee, as family.

The Thai family's home close to the Jaguar plant in Bangkok, which has a room for Robbert referred to as "Uncle's Room."

In 1995 he was again invited to Bangkok. This time he stayed in "Uncle's Room" in the newly built family home across the road from the factory. His ground floor bedroom had a king-sized bed with Robbert's photo over it. He had an ensuite bath, which was made to suit his mobility needs, as there were handles installed on the deep maroon-coloured bathtub. Ms. Teun, who is in charge of purchasing at the Jaguar plant in Bangkok, said that she often prepared his room in pink because it was such a sweet colour. He sat in the same chair at the large, round dining table so he could watch the CNN financial updates and check Fairfax Financial's stock price. He was always thankful for his accommodations, which he termed "The Hotel Jaguar," to which he gave a six-star rating.

Robbert loved oysters and the fruit available in Thailand. He was not afraid to experiment with the food; however, he was cautious to try only small amounts of new things. Sornchai brought Robbert to a good restaurant one evening and Robbert ate two or three pieces of raw oyster. He enjoyed the oysters, but his stomach was quite upset after the meal. Sornchai took Robbert to the hospital and took care of everything for him. Robbert loved having someone be so considerate of his needs and he appreciated the treatment very much.

Robbert (right) enjoying a Thai dish with Sornchai (left).

Robbert wrote to CESO in 1996 to explain his experiences in Thailand. He said, "It is often not possible to know what happens to a client after one leaves but when it is possible to learn what took place, it is a real joy for a VA — and when that VA remains part of the Family, it makes it all so much worthwhile." Robbert, Sornchai, and his sons exchanged faxes regularly and Jaguar was first on Robbert's speed dial on his fax machine. For all of his correspondence to them, Robbert signed, "Your Uncle Robbert."

Sornchai and his family kept in regular communication. Robbert even met with Sornchai in Italy to review machinery in which Jaguar was interested. The two men also travelled together to Hong Kong and Singapore on business. In 1997, after completing his bachelor's degree in Thailand, Rittichai planned to improve his English skills by taking language courses before applying for his Master of Business Administration (MBA) in North America. Robbert contacted Georgian College about language training, and with his guidance Rittichai went to the Barrie campus to study English as a second language for eight months. During that time he often saw Robbert for dinner or to run an errand together. Robbert offered to buy Rittichai a second-hand car, but he refused.

A proud "Uncle Robbert" at Akachai's graduation in Wisconsin (above) and Rittichai's graduation in Arizona (below).

By 1998, Robbert had made six trips to Thailand since his first CESO assignment in 1989. In December of that year, Akachai and Rittichai visited Robbert in Canada and they had dinner at Bayview Gardens, in Richmond Hill. Akachai was then working on his PhD in engineering at the University of Wisconsin-Madison. In May 2000, Robbert attended Akachai's graduation in Wisconsin, along with Sornchai, Suchitra, and Rittichai. They went to Akachai's supervisor's house for dinner following the ceremony, and Uncle Robbert was included in all of the family celebrations. Later that year, Robbert attended Rittichai's MBA graduation in Arizona. Both Akachai and Rittichai were honoured to have Robbert as their guest at such important occasions.

After completing their degrees, Akachai and Rittichai became involved in managing the family business and began taking on more responsibilities. Sornchai was reluctant at first to allow his sons the freedom to control aspects of Jaguar. Robbert convinced Sornchai that this transition was essential. After spending two days and nights thinking about a letter Sornchai had sent, addressing this issue, Robbert replied, "It is recognized that the founder-entrepreneur, like you, is extremely difficult to replace (and yet none of us are going to live forever!). To allow the business to live beyond his lifetime he must become more flexible, more forward-looking, more willing to change, with age. To achieve that requires wisdom." Sornchai only completed his education to grade four and he worked hard all of his life to build Jaguar Industries. Robbert acknowledged that successful businessmen have gotten along very well without a master's degree. "The University of Real Work' is often by far the best education," said Robbert. "I also know from personal experience that it is not easy to give someone else the freedom to act (perhaps differently than we would have done), but it is essential to give [your sons] that liberty."

Robbert embraced the role of uncle, and his letters to Sornchai and his sons are that of a family member, rather than an advisor. In November 2001 he wrote to Sornchai and said, "As you know I am personally emotionally very much interested in the continuing success of Jaguar and will gladly do whatever I can to see Jaguar prosper in the future as it has done in the past."

Robbert's letters and his words always encouraged Jaguar's growth and progress. He wrote, "To develop all talents, one needs to be able to have the freedom to try new ideas, even make some mistakes, because that is how people grow. It would be completely wrong to expect the next generation to be exactly like the older generation — progress requires that they are different." This advice, and the Jaguar family's hard work, fostered the company's tremendous growth since Robbert first visited in 1989. Sornchai and his family were grateful for Robbert's mentoring. In May 2000 Sornchai wrote Robbert, saying,

> I've realized it is unbelievable that I can do up to this level. There are many things that Uncle taught me. I recognize them all and apply as well, never expect that it would be so great. I think god help me. In my mind, there are many gods but you are the one who have helped and taught me. I can recognize all of your recommendations. However, I don't know how to renumerate your goodness. Even for the air-ticket, you did not allow me to pay. All your goodness will be in my heart forever, I hope god bless you with healthy. And not so long, hope I can see you again.

Robbert would not allow Sornchai to pay for any of his expenses, and Sornchai would never allow Robbert to pay for anything during his stays in Thailand. It was a continual battle between the two of them to show their appreciation, and both men were very strong-minded and refused to allow the other to pay. At one hotel, the two men vied with one another for about 15 minutes when trying to pay for the rooms. Sornchai and Robbert wanted to provide for one another, so when Thailand was hit by a recession in the 1990s, Robbert offered to invest in Jaguar, but Sornchai did not want to impose on him to help out financially. Suchitra explained that when Robbert went on the CESO assignment in 1989 he was supposed to receive 10,000 Thai baht for his services, but Robbert refused and told Sornchai to invest 9,000 Thai baht as the first investment capital in Jaguar. Sornchai refused, because he felt Robbert had already done enough. Robbert insisted and said to take the investment or else he would not return to help. Other than this Sornchai and Robbert did not exchange money and this made for a relationship without financial complications or strings attached.

They did not have the same culture, or the same background — they did not even speak the same language, but Robbert and Sornchai were hard-working men who respected one another. "They have something in common, but they are also different in terms of running a business," said Rittichai. Robbert appreciated Sornchai because he would listen and follow through with his recommendations. Robbert would usually leave a list of about ten things to do, and it gave him an excuse to come back and

Top: Akachai and Robbert discussing Jaguar business in Robbert's home in Perkinsfield.

Below: Robbert's nephew J.J. Schokking, Robbert, and Akachai.

see the results. If there was nothing done, he would not make the trip because he did not want to waste the Jaguar staff's time. Both men could see the improvements each year when Robbert would visit. Sornchai wrote Robbert, saying, "I always thank you for your advice. The most sure thing is that, in this world, I respect your knowledge, your capability, and your idea the most in the world. You are in my mind and in my admiration everyday respectfully." In another letter he said, "I pray for you before I go to work and before I go to bed to give you happiness perfectly forever. I love and respect you very much and hope to see you coming soon."

Robbert always had an open invitation to visit Bangkok and he was invited to both Akachai's and Rittichai's weddings. He prepared a speech for the latter occasion in which he poked fun at the groom for being seasick on his boat one summer. The two of them were on D'eendracht together and Rittichai ate too much one night, causing him to be ill on board. Robbert loved to tease him every chance he could about his weak sea legs. In October 2002, Akachai and Rittichai stayed with Robbert in Midland for a week to discuss Jaguar business. The week was scheduled to address Jaguar's progress and future actions. He taught Rittichai accounting techniques while they were there. He would challenge them in business to push them towards the goals they set for Jaguar. As Robbert enjoyed cooking very much, he often cooked during the week for his guests.

Robbert liked his trips to Thailand to be structured and he liked to use his time effectively, for both work and weekend excursions. Akachai would often send him a draft itinerary for the trip. Everything from meeting particulars, to weekend vacations, to "free time" was scheduled in advance. "Everyone knew he was so punctual," said Rittichai. Robbert would often be ready 15 minutes early just to make sure he was on time. When Robbert went to Thailand, Sornchai and his family made the most of Robbert's expertise and companionship. After initially meeting with Sornchai, Robbert would tour the factory to observe changes made since his last visit as well as visiting a few of the expanding Jaguar factories. The employees heard Robbert was a wealthy man, but they were surprised when he arrived in an old shirt.

He met with employees from various departments of Jaguar (including production, purchasing, accounting, manufacturing, export, engineering, and marketing) who presented problems to him for his advice. Every sector of Jaguar would be involved with Robbert. On the November 2001 itinerary, for example, Ms. Kanokon Sirinimitphol made a presentation on "The progression of personnel department"; Ms. Wanpen Jiratikul presented "Material procurement for production"; and Mr. Puntip Kanpackdee presented "Cutting layout problem and how to improve it" — just three examples of about a dozen presentations during that trip. During the meetings Robbert would sit and listen to the information. He would analyze the people to understand where they were coming from with the issue. If he could, Robbert would answer on the spot, but if he did not know the answer, he might take a day or two to think about it before giving advice. Ms. Supee, in human resources at the Bangkok factory, said that when Robbert came, he was always concerned with asking the department heads, "What's next?" She worked with Robbert every year during the last ten years.

The Jaguar employees participating in dance aerobics before the workday.

Sornchai was not well educated in human resources; therefore, he did not understand how to adequately provide sufficient salary and benefits to his employees. Robbert explained to him that the only way to keep staff

Above and Below: Jaguar employees at the Chon Buri plant.

was to give them money to survive each day. He believed in incentives for employees as well. On his advice, a library was set up in the Bangkok factory to allow employees the opportunity to read newspapers or books during their breaks. Many of the employees remembered Robbert's smile and helpful nature during his visits. Ms. Chilaluck, in charge of accounting at the Bangkok factory, said that Robbert always gave knowledge to her and everyone else. She said he had a good heart and it was from the soul. He had a generous spirit and he gave more than he received.

Robbert would always pass along encouraging words to motivate the staff. The employees at Jaguar still refer to Robbert as "Uncle" and they respect his advice and knowledge. Ms. Teun said, "Everyone loved Uncle because he was one of our family." Due to a recession, Robbert advised Ms. Teun to compare costs from multiple countries rather than importing and exporting only to one country. He followed up with her a year later and remembered what they had discussed. Ms. Nongyao, a production manager at the Bangkok plant, wrote Robbert, asking him questions about production and lazy employees. To her surprise, Robbert responded to her letter with advice to motivate workers. Robbert explained to Mr. Sinlert, assistant general manager at the Bangkok factory, that you could have the best machines and the best material, but the experienced worker is most important.

During one visit, in appreciation for his help, the Jaguar employees gave Robbert a Jaguar shirt. They were excited to see him in it the next day. Robbert joked about having sent Akachai a picture of him wearing a shirt that the Jaguar employees had given him, standing in front of his Jaguar car. He said, "Around the end of the year I have to go to the Caribbean, to show off my special shirt." Robbert was always touched by the kindness and hospitality of Jaguar.

Mr. Phanthipe, who was in charge of night production at the Bangkok plant, said that Robbert saw the difficult as easy. He had the knowledge and the know-how to help Jaguar employees with various issues. When there were bottlenecks in the production line, Robbert asked if Jaguar would ever consider increasing shift lengths. Overtime or hiring more people was more efficient than buying more machines. Labour is inexpensive in Thailand; therefore, Jaguar uses some automatic machines and conveyors, but much of the work is still done manually because it is affordable and effective. Robbert met with dozens of employees personally to answer

questions, but all of the factory workers knew "Uncle Robbert" when he came. The trip would conclude with final recommendations from Robbert and the traditional farewell dinner with the Jaguar family.

With Robbert's help, Jaguar Industries became an important Thai producer of stainless steel flatware and hollowware. Jaguar Industries has four locations in Thailand. The Bangkok location employs approximately 195 people and produces more than 60,000 spoons, forks, and knives with a mirror finish a day for domestic use and for export. In the Chon Buri location, east of Bangkok, there are an average of 200 employees and the factory produces more than 300,000 spoons and forks for domestic and export. They also do deep drawing, such as pots and pans, and manufacture more than 4,500 pieces per day. In Mae Sod, near the border of Myanmar, Jaguar has 200 employees who make more than 250,000 spoons and forks for domestic sales. The Thai Sato Tableware factory employs about 130 people and makes more than 50,000 spoons and forks for export only. Jaguar makes 99 per cent of the flatware that says "Made in Thailand" (whether it is labelled as such or under a company that buys Jaguar products). The company "grew quickly under its entrepreneurial founder — and achieved stability and the proper controls with the knowledge of the second generation of this family-owned business," wrote Robbert.

Robbert's advice and dedication to Jaguar saw the business through tremendous growth and success.

Bottom: Jaguar showroom located near the Bangkok plant.

Top: Robbert enjoying a break with Sornchai and Suchitra while sightseeing.

Middle: Conversing with a guide during the tour.

Bottom: Suchitra, Rasamee, Robbert, Sornchai, and Rittichai at Angkor Wat.

天心遺愛慈仁孝義揚家國

Robbert posing during a day
trip in Thailand.

"Having achieved so much in a short period augurs well for the future
growth of this enterprise. It has been my pleasure to see this company grow
and prosper over the last ten years."

Robbert continued to visit Thailand into his 80s. He tried not to let his
age hold him back, but he had asthma and other health problems which
made it difficult for him to walk long distances. In 2003, Sornchai offered to
take him to Angkor Wat, in Cambodia, an ancient Hindu temple complex.
Robbert was hesitant because of his health, but visiting Angkor Wat was
a long-standing wish — dating back to 1932. He went to Cambodia and he
walked some and then rested, but he thoroughly enjoyed the sites. Robbert
did not like to have his picture taken, so he was surprised that Thai people
took so many pictures, and he could not avoid it at such a beautiful site

as Angkor Wat. When Sornchai offered another trip in 2004, Robbert replied, "I know that I have deteriorated physically (I walk slower, take more rests, etc. — which is necessary with my atrial fibrillation, which means taking each day a fair dose of rat poisoning). To my great pleasure it has not prevented me from continuing my work (which I continue to enjoy greatly)."

Over the years it started to take a little more time for Robbert to recuperate from the long trips to Thailand. As he got older he took approximately a week to recover. He gladly continued his trips, but he began to cut back on any extra excursions that required much physical activity. Robbert did not want anyone to touch him while he walked, if he was having difficulties. He would say, "If I want you to help, I will tell you."

Robbert planned a trip to Thailand in the fall of 2006. That September, Sornchai passed away. Robbert postponed his trip out of respect for the family's mourning and religious services. He went to Thailand later that year to help Suchitra, Akachai and Rittichai cope with their loss, and he guided them through this troubled time. With Sornchai's death, Robbert lost a family member and he continued to mentor Jaguar Industries to honour Sornchai. Akachai and Rittichai were entrusted with new responsibilities and they often sought Robbert's business advice. Rittichai wrote to him, saying, "My dad Sornchai often told me to believe in what you say because he mentioned that no one in our family is as smart and knowledgeable as you are. He felt so lucky to meet you, and so do I."

Robbert reflecting on the beautiful scenery during a day trip.

After Sornchai passed away, Akachai approached Robbert with the idea of setting up a foundation to honour his father and Robbert. The RSJ (Robbert, Sornchai, Jaguar) Foundation was set up with funds contributed by Robbert and Jaguar. Robbert donated money to the foundation, which was founded to provide scholarship funds and research funding, to support employee welfare of the Jaguar company and to share with other organizations to help the public. The aim was to fund students who would come to Jaguar to work after graduation or who would go back to their hometowns to work. Akachai wanted Hartog in the name of the foundation, but Robbert refused.

On Friday January 25, 2008, Akachai called Robbert and said that Jaguar had to improve quality because the company had an inspection coming up. Robbert said the company needed to focus on quality

Sornchai and Robbert at a Buddhist temple.

to survive. Akachai agreed. After this conversation, Robbert mentioned to his nephew J.J. Schokking that the company finally gets it. He tried for years to convince Sornchai to focus on quality and Akachai understood the value in this. Robbert planned to go to Bangkok in March 2008 to visit with the Jaguar family and discuss the progress of the business. Akachai and Rittichai arranged to get a golf cart in order to make travelling around the factories easier for Robbert. The family and the employees at Jaguar looked forward to his visit.

CHAPTER ELEVEN

Final Days

On the morning of Thursday, January 24, 2008, Robbert fell on an icy patch in a parking lot in Midland just as he was getting organized to attend a municipal council meeting to discuss items relating to the Shelter Now project. Reinhart Weber arrived there shortly after Robbert to join him in the meeting and found him sitting on the ground in the parking lot. Reinhart, with the help of a man from the neighbourhood assisted Robbert to his feet, but Robbert, in his typical style, insisted that the meeting go on (which was likely beneficial for the meeting, as they were able to clear all of the issues presented that morning). When the meeting was done, an ambulance took Robbert to the hospital where Reinhart waited with him until he was given medical treatment.

Early that afternoon J.J. Schokking , Robbert's nephew picked him up from the hospital. J.J. had moved to Midland from Holland in 2002 to assist Robbert who found it increasingly more difficult to drive in his old age. This time the doctors concluded that he had broken his shoulder. Those close to Robbert knew that his independence was important to him and Robbert and J.J. spent the next few days in the house, with Robbert staying active, fielding calls and reading.

On Sunday January 27th, Robbert, J.J., his daughter Anne, along with his nephew Ronald and his wife Lisa, had lunch together. This was followed by a long talk between Robbert and Ronald. After the visitors left, Robbert watched the finals of the Australian Open tennis tournament that had been played earlier that day as J.J. prepared one of Robbert's favourite dinners. Robbert suddenly suffered a heart attack.

Robbert's neighbour, Stephen Lalonde, had just sat down to relax for the evening after clearing about four feet of snow and ice from his property, he noticed an ambulance go by the front of his house and then come back, driving slowly. He saw the ambulance at the bottom of Robbert's driveway, which has a steep incline and was slippery and snowy. Stephen did not think the ambulance could make it to Robbert's home, so he quickly got into his four-wheel drive Buick Rendezvous and drove over to assist. Stephen and the paramedics drove up Robbert's driveway and were greeted at the door by J.J. They explained to J.J. and Robbert that the ambulances did not have snow tires and the paramedics transferred Robbert to a chair they use occasionally for transports. "We proceeded outside to my vehicle, I opened the passenger side door," Stephen recalled. "Mr. Hartog had to stand up to do the transfer from chair to vehicle. He then winked at me, then he was seated in the vehicle."

As Stephen drove down the driveway to the ambulance, Robbert lost consciousness and the paramedics began performing CPR. At the bottom of the driveway the paramedics transferred Robbert to the ambulance, but his Do Not Resuscitate order was respected. With that, Robbert Hartog's life's work came to an end. With a wink and a nod he was gone.

Postscript

What does one contemplate in one's final moments? Perhaps Robbert's mind returned to his happy youth, frolicking at Versailles; perhaps his mind's eye gazed over the sun-dappled waters of Georgian Bay, or drank in the grand vistas of the northern Canadian wilderness; did he return to the lushness of Thailand, or soar around the world he had experienced?; did his thoughts turn to family and friends, his business triumphs, his charitable and community works? We can never know, of course, but all these things and so much more made up the sum of the man who was Robbert Hartog. Word of Robbert's death spread quickly to people in all areas of his life throughout the world. While his loss was to be mourned, this was also an opportunity for his life to be celebrated. On Thursday, January 31, 2008, a clear and crisp evening in Midland, friends and family gathered at Brooklea Golf and Country Club to celebrate Robbert. Hundreds of people filled the venue to its capacity to share stories and listen to speeches by family members, friends, and representatives from his various charitable and business endeavours. True to Robbert's legacy, all of the speakers were asked to keep their words brief.

Robbert's wishes were the main emphasis for his memorial services. During discussions after his death, it became apparent that no one was certain about his decision for burial or cremation. The events were organized around a future burial, as it was midwinter in snow-covered Midland. Months later, as his nephew J.J. Schokking was cleaning out Robbert's desk, he came across a note in Robbert's handwriting that expressed his wish to be cremated and have his ashes scattered over some of his favourite places, including Georgian Bay. Some of Robbert's ashes were also sent to Thailand. They are under a picture of him in a shrine dedicated to Robbert and Sornchai at the Bangkok factory. The wall of the shrine features a copper mural of Sornchai's journey in business. Robbert is pictured with Sornchai handing him a bag of money; however, the image symbolizes the knowledge that Robbert passed on to help Jaguar Industries flourish. The employees of Jaguar pray to the shrine daily.

Upon hearing of Robbert's passing, members of the Thai family immediately made travel arrangements to Ontario and they attended the funeral on Friday, February 1. That morning a snowstorm hit Midland and the town was engulfed with flurries as Robbert's community made its way to St. Paul's United Church. Robbert's nephews Ronald and J.J. Schokking said, "Notwithstanding the weather Robbert would not have approved of starting late; thus the service started on time." Cliff Pendlebury and Robbert's sister Rose-Marjan Hartog officiated at the service. His friend Fred Hacker and Robbert's nephew Michael Mansell (Ellen and Oliver's son) delivered words of remembrance.

At the beginning of Michael's speech he quoted Robbert's obituary: "Robbert, paterfamilias par excellence, is survived by his sister Rose-Marjan Hartog and his ten nieces and nephews; he was predeceased by his sister Ellen and his brother Dolf." He explained that "on the face of it, it might seem strange that a life-long bachelor should be called a 'paterfamilias' but for Robbert the description couldn't be better. He made a point of keeping in touch, and for our family branch of Arthur's descendants he was the focal point for an annual get-together, which takes some doing as his ten nephews and nieces live in seven different countries on three continents."

Robbert's nieces and nephews remembered him as a father at large, a teacher, a mentor, and a guide (on Georgian Bay and through life's obstacles). His nephew Claude Mansell referred to him as a "bringer of comfort in times of difficulties and sorrow," and referenced a time when he was experiencing personal trouble. "Suddenly, looking outside into our street in The Hague in The Netherlands," Claude said, "I saw this wise man, Robbert, who had come totally unexpectedly from Canada to stand by. A 24-hour trip to help out at exactly the right moment." Robbert's nephew Arthur Hartog remembered Robbert's daily phone calls to his father Dolf when his health was failing. Arthur said, "Robbert felt that a call in the morning might help my father through the day and because of the time difference [Dolf lived in France], he set his alarm clock to some awfully early time of the night to catch my father when he woke up." Bryan Schokking recalled Robbert's humour as an eight-year-old Bryan bugged his uncle for a cigar. After much begging, Robbert gave in and gave him a cigar. Soon, Bryan was sick from his new experience. Robbert came in his room to check on the ailing boy and Bryan said, "He came in smoking a big cigar and smiling!" Beatrice Brom (formerly Mansell) appreciated Robbert's role in her children's life as he flew to Israel for their weddings and welcomed their husbands to the extended family. "It was extremely meaningful for me to have him there, representing my mother, who passed away many years before," said Beatrice. Robbert was very close to her father, Oliver, who was in very bad health when Robbert passed. When informed of the news, Oliver told the doctor, "I have just lost my best friend." A week later he passed away.

Beatrice also recalled Robbert's visits to their family's home in Holland. Her mother (and Robbert's sister), Ellen, always provided Dutch herring that was not available in Canada or New York, and jenever (Dutch gin). The visits were a whirlwind, but Beatrice was always excited to spend time with Robbert. Yvonne Mansell remembered Robbert's visits over the years: "He would connect with each of us, asking questions about our music or sports, our school and friends, and even though he didn't spend a long time, because of how he related to us, the connection was real." Robbert valued his family and time spent with them, as Rose-Marjan explained, he "made it his social task to give his love to those who needed it. His nieces and nephews felt that. It wasn't only that he helped them; he talked to them … He knew everyone's traits, when to help, when not to help."

Robbert's family gathered to pay tribute to him in his adopted Canadian homeland and many were shocked at the reception he received. Not being one to seek recognition, Robbert did not often speak of his contributions in his community and throughout the world. Many who gathered during those cold winter days in Midland, from all areas of Robbert's life, found themselves at one time saying, "I didn't know Robbert was involved with that," referring to numerous organizations and causes with which Robbert was so passionately involved.

After the church service, Robbert's casket, under police escort, travelled through the town that had meant so much to him and benefited so much from his presence. Robbert's legacy is visible throughout the town — from buildings erected through his efforts, to the citizens partaking in the programs he supported. Even his final wishes reflected his support for the community — he requested memorial donations to the Huronia Hospitals Foundation. Members of organizations and fundraising initiatives in Midland felt an immediate loss with Robbert's passing; yet, his spirit of innovation, community, and education continues to thrive.

Traces of Robbert's ongoing legacy can be found throughout Midland. Community Living Huronia used posthumous support from Robbert to complete the purchase of a new building in downtown Midland to house their Supported Employment and Supported Independent Living programs. Funds were also used to support children and teen summer programs run by the organization. Wendat set plans in motion to purchase a new building to expand its services and created a sustainability fund to generate interest revenue for daily operating costs. St. Paul's Church plans to use some of the money from Robbert's bequest for an organ/sanctuary renovation project. The Wye Marsh Wildlife Centre created the Robbert

Hartog Environmental Education (Enhancement) Fund to expand the opportunities for students across Ontario to learn and understand the importance of conservation and preservation. Robbert's legacy will also "enable the Wye Marsh to increase its capacity to take environmental stewardship to another level," commented Laurie Schutt, executive director of the Wye Marsh. "Through balanced and thoughtful growth the Friends of the Wye Marsh will invest in the stewardship of the Wye Marsh and the Wye Valley, will increase its technological capabilities to educate a whole new audience, improve/upgrade facilities … and develop a strong volunteer and staff base." The YMCA of Simcoe/Muskoka established the Robbert Hartog YMCA Scholarship Fund with part of his legacy, to create an endowment to support one or more students in financial need who wish to pursue post-secondary education in an area of study that could lead to a career in the YMCA. The remainder of his gift will be used to support the construction of the new YMCA within Simcoe/Muskoka.

The Huronia Hospitals Foundation formed the Robbert Hartog-Gil Robillard Advisory Committee in April 2008 to honour the legacy of philanthropy of two of the foundation's lifetime members. The committee will bring together community members who are dedicated to the foundation's mission and understand the importance of fundraising. Huronia Hospitals Foundation president Kathy Befort said, "It is our hope that by naming the committee after them, it will be one way their spirit of caring will live on." In May 2009, the Huronia Hospitals Foundation established the Robbert Hartog Innovation in Health Care Fund. "This fund is for today's needs," said Kathy. "It will support new equipment honouring Robbert's ongoing reminder that hospital donations advance technology and provide for innovation in care. This will continue Robbert's vision of making our hospital the best community hospital in the province."

Since Robbert's death, his friend and fellow philanthropist Reinhart Weber continued to support Shelter Now through the completion of its construction at 850 Hartman Drive in Midland. Reinhart and Robbert felt strongly about the initiative from the beginning. Shelter Now was a symbol of Robbert's generosity and community leadership and Reinhart felt this particular work should be acknowledged. With the support of Reinhart and the blessing of Robbert's family, the organizers of Shelter Now honoured Robbert's dedication to the project by naming the housing unit "Hartog House." Robbert's friends and family gathered at the grand opening of the facility on June 26, 2009.

On August 22, 2008, the Midland Georgian College Campus (and former Industrial Research and Development Institute building) was renamed the "Robbert Hartog Midland Campus" to honour Robbert's legacy with Georgian College. "The Robbert Hartog Midland Campus is without a doubt one of the finest Skilled Trades Centres in Canada," commented Brian Tamblyn, the president of Georgian College. "As events have unfolded over the past decade, and with the benefit of hindsight, the gradual conversion of IRDI into a Skilled Trades Centre and a local post-secondary campus was timely, necessary, and impactful. The campus will literally change the lives of thousands of students for the better for many years to come, an outcome that Robbert would be proud of."

Robbert's legacy also impacted the University of Waterloo, where his support is being used to enhance the presence of the Faculty of Engineering on campus. In 2007, after discussing plans for a Student Design Centre in a new engineering building with Dean of Engineering Adel Sedra, Robbert explained that he would make a provision in his will for the University to see the project through. "It is, therefore, quite befitting his legacy that his bequest be applied towards an area at the University of Waterloo that has inspired Robbert during his lifetime," reflected Dean Sedra. "Robbert's contribution to the construction of the Mechanical and Mechatronics research labs in [Engineering V] is significant. In recognition of this, we will name a research wing on the third floor in his honour. This research wing will provide leading-edge research space for our enterprising and high calibre researchers doing innovative work in areas such as robotics, biofuels and biomedical sciences, among others." Sedra further explained that the labs are "where day-to day theories and data will be tested and developed into products that will benefit society and help Canada's economic prosperity." In six stories and more than 150,000 gross square feet, Engineering V will provide mechanical and mechatronics engineering and systems design engineering with central administration offices, informal work spaces, classrooms, common rooms, workshops, and studios. The construction of the building neared completion at the end of the summer of 2009. "This lasting legacy is befitting of a man who showed so much interest in the education and research of our students, and who was a true friend and mentor of Waterloo Engineering."

Robbert had a powerful impact on his friends in Thailand at Jaguar Industries. To honour his legacy, a section of English books at the Faculty of Pharmaceutical Sciences library at the Prince of Songkla University in Hat Yai was established. The project was organized with the support of

Dean Niwat and Dr. Surachat from the Faculty of Pharmaceutical Sciences and funding from the Robbert, Sornchai, Jaguar (RSJ) Foundation. Akachai spoke with Robbert's family after his death about acquiring some of his many books he kept in his personal library. Akachai worked in a rare books section at a library in Wisconsin and during his visits to Midland while completing his graduate studies he would often talk to Robbert about his book collection. Forty-five boxes of books (with approximately one hundred books per box) were sent from Canada to Bangkok and shipped with Jaguar trucks to Hat Yai (in the south of Thailand, about an hour north of the border of Malaysia). The RSJ Foundation also donated 500,000 Thai baht to set up the library and will donate 200,000 baht each year for further educational tools and development. Some of the books in the library are fiction and will be circulated, and some rare books or encyclopedias will be available on reserve. Robbert's books will allow staff and students to enrich themselves with various topics, as well as practice and develop English reading skills. The RSJ Foundation library opened on April 29, 2009.

Robbert's legacy is alive in the many people he inspired throughout his lifetime. Several close friends have pictures of Robbert in their offices or homes. A few have the words "What Would Robbert Have Done?" inscribed below. Although Robbert lived his life anonymously, he humbly inspired others not only to achieve greatness in their own lives, but also to enable the community (both local and international) to thrive as well. Robbert's friend Fred Hacker eloquently speaks of Robbert's legacy in this final tribute:

It is a challenge to try to address the impact of Robbert Hartog. How does one summarize the life of a man with so many facets, so many qualities, so many achievements, and so many relationships? Each of us who knew him had a special connection with Robbert Hartog. And each of us who knew him has our own story to tell.

When, on the evening before his funeral, family and friends gathered to share memories, the most frequent comment, as we shared our stories, was "I never knew that about Robbert!" I learned, in the days following his death, that the Robbert I thought I knew was incredibly more complex, vastly more accomplished and remarkably more influential than I was aware. And I adored Robbert Hartog long before I learned of those added dimensions. We could provide great lists of his achievements, his recognitions, his experiences and his associations. But the impact of the man went far beyond what such lists would convey.

To really understand his impact, we have to begin with a simple but profound statement. Robbert Hartog changed lives! In everything he did, one of the results was that lives were changed — for the better. His love and guidance were powerful forces in the lives of his family, particularly for his nieces and nephews. His leadership of many Scouts and Rovers was to shape and mould those young men for life. His mentoring and encouragement were formative influences in the lives of many of us who worked with him on charitable and philanthropic ventures. His wisdom and experience were key factors in the successes of the many businesses and business leaders that he counselled — locally, nationally and internationally.

Some of the businesses that benefited from Robbert's counsel were located within miles of where Robbert made his home. One of the most successful entrepreneurs in the Midland-Penetanguishene area worried aloud following Robbert's funeral about to whom he would now turn for advice. Some of those businesses were a world away. Four people from Thailand arrived for Robbert's funeral. They were so affected by Robbert's assistance to their business in Thailand that they flew halfway around the world to pay tribute. Volunteers and executives in non-profit and community organizations learned valuable lessons from Robbert about management, marketing, finance, vision and planning. Robbert's friendship was precious for those fortunate enough to get close to him. Every friend's story is personal and special and revealing. Each of those stories has a common theme. That theme is that Robbert made a difference in the life of the story teller.

I couldn't help but reflect, as I prepared my eulogy for his funeral, on the many people who never knew Robbert Hartog, yet whose lives were profoundly affected by him. People in communities in faraway corners of the world who now have jobs and dignity because Robbert helped establish and nurture businesses. People who benefited from Robbert's contributions to international organizations. Students who have received a better education because of Robbert's commitment, leadership and financial contributions to institutions of higher learning. People whose lives will be enhanced by a healthier environment because of Robbert's interest in and support of organizations like the World Wildlife Fund and the Wye Marsh Wildlife Centre. Residents of the Midland-Penetanguishene community enjoy recreational facilities, cultural facilities, improved health care facilities and programs that offer care, support and hope to people.

Our community is a better place because of Robbert Hartog. We have industries, an industrial research facility, a post-secondary education campus, a spectacular YMCA, an exceptional wildlife centre, a quality hospital, and facilities and programs too numerous to mention. And much of the credit for those facilities must go to Robbert Hartog — for his leadership, encouragement, guidance, determination and financial contributions.

I've referred to the philanthropy of Robbert Hartog. Robbert never wanted anyone to say anything about that aspect of his life. He never wanted recognition for his remarkable generosity. He always wanted to be the anonymous donor. At his funeral, I told this story. A few years ago, an individual (not Robbert) made a donation to a local community organization. When asked how the acknowledgment should read, the individual replied: "Just mark it 'Anonymous Donor.'" I had to explain to the individual that that designation was already permanently taken in our community!

It's easy to look at the achievements of Robbert Hartog and conclude that he contributed in "big ways." But he also contributed to each of us in small but important ways. He taught us to care — to care about people we might never meet. He taught us the importance of preparation, of foresight and of planning. He taught us that people of faith, integrity, and honour can succeed on every playing field in our society. He taught us that there is only one way to do anything, and that is the "right way." No shortcuts. No half efforts. No excuses. Just get it done. And do it right! He taught us that obstacles in our paths are minor inconveniences, not barriers. He taught us that values and moral standards never go out of style. He taught us that you can have fun while achieving important objectives. He taught us that there is not a meeting worth attending that shouldn't be wrapped up in 59 minutes.

In my eulogy, I shared a fond memory of Robbert. For the last few summers of Robbert's life, my wife, Barb, and I had taken Robbert for a boat ride on his beloved Georgian Bay. The summer before his death, we went north by boat to the Sans Souci area of Georgian Bay and explored some of the anchorages that Robbert had frequented decades earlier. When it was time to head home, I asked Robbert if he was feeling adventurous. He looked at me quizzically and said (and, if you knew Robbert, you could just hear him say), "It all depends." I told Robbert that I'd like to run back to Midland down the "outside"; that is, we would head out into the middle of Georgian Bay and travel home in open waters. Now there are two things you should know. First, it was a very windy and rough day. And second, our boat is not what you would picture Robbert in. It is an offshore speedboat capable of speeds of more than 120 kilometres per hour. Robbert was game. So off we went. It was rough. As we headed south, running with the seas, the spray would occasionally come right up over the windscreen and, literally, soak us. I kept looking over at Robbert. He was hanging on for dear life. Water dripped down his face. His hair was slicked to his head. His glasses were fogged. And he was laughing out loud!

And he looked over at me with a big smile and said, "This is fun!"

Knowing Robbert and sharing just a small corner of his life was fun!

I concluded my eulogy with this:

"Robbert. How do we say farewell?

How do we thank you for all you have meant to each of us — and to the countless others who are not in this sanctuary?

I suspect if you were with us, you'd tell us that you never wanted recognition or thanks. I think you'd say it was fun and rewarding for you too.

So, what do we do, now that you're gone? What would you want us to do, Robbert?

I believe that we can best say thank you by living our lives in a manner worthy of being able to say, 'Robbert would have approved.'"

Photo Gallery

Index

Index continued